BEYOND THE DICTIONARY
IN ITALIAN

CASSELL'S

BEYOND THE DICTIONARY
IN ITALIAN

by

P. J. T. GLENDENING

FUNK & WAGNALLS
New York

CONTENTS

CONTENTS

PREFACE

The present volume follows the successful pattern of 'Beyond the Dictionary in Spanish', which appeared in 1953. The idea is to present a key to present-day living speech, such as is not to be obtained from any grammar book and which could only partly and with great difficulty and liability to error be gleaned from a comprehensive dictionary. Let us be quite clear about one thing: you can get by well enough without knowing exactly which word or expression to use in which place—indeed, some people boast of being able to make themselves understood without a word of the language—but if you want to be a cut above the person who, to refer to the Italian learner of English for clarity, says: 'I have experimented a great emotion at the announcement' for 'The announcement made me quite excited', then it is worth going deeper into the language and getting the feel of it. The object of this book is to give you this feel of the language.

I have kept to the pattern of 'Beyond the Dictionary in Spanish' in almost every respect, except that in the Miscellaneous Notes I have touched on one or two further points, while the list of Special Vocabularies is slightly different. Otherwise, as in the Spanish book, where the main part is the Spanish-English section, so here the main part is the Italian-English section, with the English-Italian section as a mere cross-reference.

Two things should be pointed out here, both stressed in 'Beyond the Dictionary in Spanish'. Firstly, this book is not a reference book of slang. The words contained here are perfectly good standard and colloquial Italian, words of everyday use in normal contexts, not jargon expressions of restricted use. Slang is a fascinating subject, but this is not the place for it. Secondly, it is hoped that this book will be referred to, dipped into, browsed in at odd moments—and not treated like just another dictionary, to be consulted only when an unknown word is encountered.

Now, *In bocca al lupo*, as one student says to another just about to sit for his examination, or 'Good luck!'

7

MISCELLANEOUS NOTES

The person reading this book will probably already have a very fair knowledge of the Italian language, of how it is pronounced and so on. For this reason it is obviously unnecessary to start right from scratch; instead, here are a number of pointers to tell you what pitfalls to avoid and what basic things you should do which you might not otherwise think of doing.

Note straight away that Italian is practically a one-country language. It is comparatively rare for foreigners to learn such languages, and the very fact of your doing so puts you many points up in their estimation. I won't claim that you can't put a foot wrong, but if you do, it doesn't matter. They are with you from the start, the Italians, as you are taking the trouble to learn their language. And although in the points which follow I have sometimes drawn attention to common English pitfalls in Italian, I must stress the advice not to bother so much about the possibility of making these mistakes that you never open your mouth. Naturally, the essential thing is to say something, even though it may not be one hundred per cent pure Italian. In quiet, private moments, just try to improve on certain things, but in public think just of expressing yourself, and not of being a perfectionist. Be one, by all means, but not all the time.

Pronunciation. You will certainly have read, or heard it stated, or noted for yourself, that Italian is a 'musical' language, that it has a heavy sing-song accent. That this is in fact so may be obscured if you hear the language spoken by an Italian with a pronounced regional accent (although note in passing that some regional and other accents are extremely musical), but if you tune in to the Italian radio or

8

listen to the voices of the announcers (or more especially the announceresses) on Italian TV, you will immediately recognize the musical accent. Such an accent in most other European languages tends to sound effeminate. The stress, falling regularly on the penultimate syllable, is indeed heavy, and you may emphasize single words as heavily as you wish, as you may also in English—but which you may absolutely not do in Spanish, for example. And although you may have the impression that Italians are very rapid speakers—and there is no denying that some speakers of the language are able to utter it at great rapidity—the fact of there being this heavy stress, as well as double consonants which have really to be sounded double, and frequent long vowel sounds, has a slowing influence on the language. Indeed, some linguists even claim that Italian is one of the slower European languages. Certainly it is a mistake to try to skip the heavy stress, just as it sounds foreign to fail to double double consonants. Remember, for instance, the difference between *capello* and *cappello*. I do not wish to exaggerate the importance of this difference in the understanding of the language, as common sense usually guides the hearer, and the meaning is almost clear anyway, but using the two words just as isolated sounds, and not in connected sentences, the doubling of the *p* is all the difference in the world between 'hair' and 'hat'. Shall I sound the obvious warning at this point? Don't overdo things—double means double, not treble. I so often hear people who are perfectly aware of the double sounding of double consonants, stressing the syllable in question to such an extent that it never seems to come to an end.

One of the principal English errors in speaking Italian is the retaining of weak forms. This is, of course, one of the faults committed by English people in pronouncing whatever other language they are learning. In Italian it comes out very readily, perhaps as Italian is also a language with heavy stress. In any group of syllables in English you will come across a certain number of them pronounced weakly. A weak syllable is one which undergoes a vowel change from the way the vowel is sounded if stressed. If the word 'borstal', for instance, had an accented final syllable, we should pronounce it 'al', whereas in fact, as it is unstressed, we say 'borst'l'. In Italian, however, vowels always retain their pure value, however much you may lay on the emphasis or however quickly you may speak. This weakening of certain vowels is a characteristic you notice even among very practised and expert English speakers of Italian. You may detect them saying kjarə'mɛnte instead of kjara'mɛnte (*chiaramente*), or pɔm'riddʒo instead of pɔme'riddʒo (*pomeriggio*) and so on. Italians understand what is being said perfectly well, but it is a nationality-betraying tendency which you may be fastidious enough to wish to try to avoid.

Remember the pronunciation of the Italian *r*-sound. Many learners make the mistake of imagining that the *r* is equally strongly rolled in Italian in all positions—and this is certainly a mistaken idea—and they then proceed to roll most strongly those *r*-sounds which come most easily to the English mouth which, in many cases, are not those *r*-sounds which should be most strongly rolled. If, for instance, you roll strongly the *r* in the infinitive ending of a verb, you are making a mistake and sound quite un-Italian. Were it intended that the infinitive *r* should be strongly rolled, it would be written with a double *r* (certain infinitives do, in fact, have *rr*, and consequent strong rolling—for example, *porre* and *trarre*). Note such differences as exist between *coro* and *corro*, and *caro* and *carro*. When there is an initial *r*, many learners find it difficult to give this sound its correct value; they then, realizing that the initial *r*-sound should be rolled and being unsuccessful in their attempt, proceed to give the next *r*-sound, if it happens to be near, the rolling of its life, regardless of whether it should be long or short. It's a sort of delayed-action roll, just as Italian learners of English, having difficulty with the *h*-sound, but being aware that it exists, will not be able to get it out in time for the first word with an *h* but will put it in when the next vowel comes along, as in: ''e his 'ere' ('he is here'). Be on your guard.

You will naturally know of the existence of the two *e*-sounds and two *o*-sounds. Confusion here is one of the surest ways for Italians to distinguish even practised foreign speakers of their language. *Pollo*, for instance, has the closed *o*-sound, while *polo* has the open *o*-sound. *Pompa* has closed *o*, *popolo* has both *o*'s. *Tortora* has initially a closed *o*, as has *torta*, while *torto* has open *o*. *Postale* has closed *o*, *posta* the open variety. Regarding the two variations of *e*, note that the closed variety is relatively common, and comes in such words as *bevere, essa, fermo, tegola*. *Telo* ('piece of cloth') is closed, but *gelo* ('cold', 'chill') is open. Lastly, I cannot resist referring to those two famous causes of confusion—*pesce* ('fish'), with initial closed *e*, and *pesca* ('peach'), with open *e*. The plural of 'fish' is *pesci* (closed *e*), the plural of 'peach' *pesche* (open *e*'s). Just to complicate matters, note also *pesca* ('fishing'), which has a closed *e*.

Diphthongs. Three points must be made here. Firstly, when two vowels are written together they do not necessarily form a diphthong—they may well be sounded separately and independently, as in *neonato*. Secondly, diphthongs are always formed with unstressed *i* or *u*. Thirdly, we divide them into two groups, according to whether the stress falls on the first element (*ai, au, ei, eu oi, ui*) or on the second element (*ia, ie, io, iu, ua, ue, ui, uo*). It must, however, be admitted that the real difficulty lies in remembering whether a vowel is stressed or unstressed. For instance, *pausa* has unstressed *u*, while *paura* has stressed *u*. Thus *pausa* has a diphthong, while *paura* has separately pronounced vowel sounds. Look at *Luigi, lui* and *buio*: *Luigi* has unstressed *u*, *lui* has stressed *u* and *buio* has stressed *u*. Again, *Italia* has unstressed *-ia*, while *Maria* and *malattia*, for example, have stressed *i*. These are by no means isolated examples, but are chosen to present the problem to you. The moral is—remember the position of the stress.

Accent. By this word we understand three separate things: stress, as referred to above; the written mark indicating stress (and variation of sound, in some languages, but not in Italian); and the regional or special way of pronouncing a language (the term 'dialect' indicates a variation of vocabulary, grammar and accent from the central language, so that accent in this sense may or may not indicate true dialect; a few sentences will generally soon demonstrate whether Italian, say, is being spoken with a regional accent, or whether a true dialect is being spoken).

Concerning the written accent, you may well be in some doubt as to which one to use and when to use it, as different grammars and dictionaries give different instructions (apart from varying usage with no explanation). Italian rules about it are really quite clear, however. Firstly, there is only one accent, the grave. Then, this accent is written as follows:

a) on words where the stress falls on the final syllable: *caffè, carità, perchè, tribù, università, virtù*;
b) on monosyllables ending in diphthongs: *già, giù, più, può* (but not on *qui* or *qua*);
c) on monosyllables which have one meaning without the accent and another one with it: for example, *da* ('from'), *dà* ('gives'); *e* ('and'), *è* ('is'); *la* ('the'), *là* ('there'); *ne* ('of it' etc.), *nè* ('neither', 'nor').

However, you know what Italians are like with rules—and far be it from me to claim that the clear rules here stated are universally adhered to. In fact, the well-known Feltrinelli paper-back series referred to as *U.E.* (*Universale Economica*) regularly uses the grave accent for *a*, most *e*'s and *o*, while the acute accent is used for the *i* and the *u*, and for such *e*'s as those in *per sé, perché, né* and so on.

In conclusion, note also that such words as *popolo, unico* and *veneto*, which are not stressed regularly (regular stress meaning the penultimate syllable, with variations noted above), do *not* take any written accent, except in some dictionaries and guides to pronunciation, which point out that you say *'popolo, 'unico* and *'veneto*. In this respect Italian differs from Spanish.

Diminutives, Augmentatives, Superlative, etc. The diminutive, although frequently employed, is not so frequent as in Spanish. Most often there is an idea of smallness, quite logically, or of something endearing, pleasant, nice. The augmentative, on the other hand, often gives the idea of something rather or very unpleasant. Over-use or wrong use of the diminutive sounds rather silly, and wrong use of the augmentative either a bit ridiculous or downright rude. In all cases, be careful. For a 'small book', why not say *piccolo libro*, for instance? Don't play about with *librino*, *libretto* and so on. If you do, you will often be using, not just the wrong word, but a confusing one. *Libretto*, for instance, apart from meaning the 'words' in opera, means 'official book required for workers' (*libretto di lavoro*). I could, but do not intend to, give a list of the various diminutives and the large number of augmentatives. Far better to learn them joined on to specific words, as *casella* ('pigeonhole', *casella postale* being 'box number'), *pochino* ('a little', 'small amount'), *prestino* (as in *È arrivato un po' prestino*, 'He's come a bit early'), *carino* ('nice', 'pretty').

A short time ago I heard someone complaining that every time he ordered a *cappuccino* (coffee with some milk added) in his local 'bar', the barman said *Sì, un cappuccio*, while, when he varied the order and said *Un cappuccio* the barman said, rather disdainfully it seemed, *Va bene, un cappuccino*— which just showed, this man contended, that the barman was determined for him to be wrong. There may be another explanation, but in any case you will find that it is indeed easy to be wrong, so once again, tread warily, but don't let this kind of thing discourage you.

Note the change of certain nouns by the addition of *–one*. The word automatically becomes both masculine and bigger — *scarpa* becoming *scarpone*, for instance, while *librone* comes from *libro*.

Just two more points. The superlative ending, *–issimo*, is of very frequent occurrence. In answer to the question: *Era interessante?* you may get, for instance, *Sì, molto interessante* or *Interessantissimo*. You would do well to cultivate the *–issimo* habit. And lastly, remember that Italian allows the repeating of adjectives to strengthen the idea. *È cattivo, cattivo* means that he is naughtier or more wicked than just plain *cattivo*. In practice you will probably come across this doubling most often with a) short adjectives, b) adjectives denoting size—and especially the latter. *Lungo lungo*, *piccolo piccolo*, *alto alto* and so forth.

How to address and refer to people. You may be be-wildered on this fundamental point, as so much contrary advice is given. Regarding how to address people, there is no difficulty about using *tu*, which is used in the same circumstances in which most other languages use their second person singular personal pronoun. Again, addressing children etc., the plural form to use is *voi*. But here the complications arise, apparently. One book I have looked at recently says: '*Voi* is the universal word for the English "you", whether one person or more is referred to.' A second book says: '*Voi, Lei* and *Loro* are the three words to translate "you", but as *Lei* and *Loro* present certain difficulties, we shall restrict ourselves here to using *Voi*.' Both are wrong, the former more so than the latter. A third book (*La Lingua Italiana*, by Roncari & Brighenti, published by Edizioni Scolastiche Mondadori, Milan), puts the position more accurately; its argument may be summarized as follows:

Voi, plural of *tu*;

Lei, normal form of address in the singular (using third person singular verb form);

Loro, normal form of address in the plural (using third person plural verb form);

Voi, used variously in addressing one or more persons, takes the second person plural verb form and is used in commercial language, among artists and in certain regions of Italy.

The only comment I have here is that it seems to be a bit of a toss-up regarding *Voi* and *Loro* meaning 'you' (plural idea). Some Italians will swear it is predominantly the one and others vice versa.

Similarly, although many books use exclusively *egli, ella* and *esso* for 'he', 'she' and 'it' respectively, with the plural forms *essi, esse* and *loro*, in actual fact you will almost every-where and always hear the verb used without any pronoun at all. Note that *lei*, meaning 'she', usually takes a small letter, when not beginning a sentence, while *Lei*, meaning 'you', is capitalized. Similarly, plural 'you' takes a capital, *Loro*.

Imperative. Here are tables showing exactly where each form of the imperative comes from:

AUXILIARIES		-*are* VERBS		-*ere* AND -*ire* VERBS
sing.	1 —	1 —		1 —
	2 special form	2 special form		2 pres. indic.
	3 pres. subj.	3 pres. subj.		3 pres. subj.
plur.	1 pres. subj.	1 pres. subj.		1 pres. subj.
	2 pres. subj.	2 pres. indic.		2 pres. indic.
	3 pres. subj.	3 pres. subj.		3 pres. subj.

N.B. The first person plural of the present tense is identical in the indicative and the subjunctive.

Thus:

avere	*essere*	*fermare*	*sentire*
sing.			
1 —	1 —	1 —	1 —
2 *abbi*	2 *sii* or *sia*	2 *ferma*	2 *senti*
3 *abbia*	3 *sia*	3 *fermi*	3 *senta*
plur.			
1 *abbiamo*	1 *siamo*	1 *fermiamo*	1 *sentiamo*
2 *abbiate*	2 *siate*	2 *fermate*	2 *sentite*
3 *abbiano*	3 *siano*	3 *fermino*	3 *sentano*

On a bus, for instance, you may hear someone, wishing to get off and being unable to do so on account of the closed door, asking the driver to open it by saying either *apra* or *aprite* according to whether this person uses the *Lei* or *Voi* form—usually one hears the *Lei* form.

Note that to give a negative command—'Don't . . .'— you add *non* to the forms shown above, except in the case of the second person singular (*tu*), when the infinitive form is used after the word *non*. Thus: 'Don't do . . .' is *Non fare* . . ., 'Don't close the door', is *Non chiuder la porta*, and 'Don't believe . . .' is *Non credere*. . . . Also, in instructions, public notices etc., the infinitive is used, both affirmatively and negatively (in these cases the understood, but mostly unexpressed, pronoun is *si*, not *tu*), as much as the *Voi* form of the imperative. Examination instructions may tell you to *scrivere* or *scrivete*, to *non dimenticare* or *non dimenticate*.

Basic constructions. It is worth while pointing out that you should be quite sure of the ground you are building on before you build. So many people go astray by learning strange words before basic vocabulary, and by trying to use complicated idioms before they know the elementary grammar of the language. I know an Englishman, resident in Italy for 23 years and married to an Italian, whom I heard, during the two hours or so of an evening meal in a restaurant, make mistakes in the grammar of the order he gave the waiter not to bring something, in the 'both . . . and . . .' construction and in giving the date. Which is quite something, after 23 years. You must be perfectly conversant with the basic sentence pattern, constructions, dates and so on. Here is a list.

più . . . (e) più . . .	the more . . . the more . . .
meno . . . (e) meno . . .	the less . . . the less . . .
sia . . . sia . . .	both . . . and . . .
nè . . . nè . . .	neither . . . nor . . .
o . . . o	either . . . or . . .
appena . . . quando . . .	hardly . . . when . . .
più . . . di . . .	more . . . than . . .
meno . . . di . . .	less . . . than . . .

Never be afraid of reading or saying numbers, however complicated they may look. Practise them to yourself. Whenever you read a date, really read it and don't skim over it. Get into the habit of doing this and numbers, both cardinal and ordinal, will soon become easy. Remember that dates take cardinal numbers, except the first of the month, which is the *primo*. For instance, 'the tenth of July' is *il dieci luglio*. On the other hand, kings, popes and so on take ordinal numbers. 'Pope John the 23rd' is referred to as *Papa Giovanni Vigesimoterzo*, and not *Ventitreesimo*, or *Ventesimoterzo*,, but here the old form is better. One last thing, don't be at a loss to know how to ask the time. I have known some quite good speakers of Italian be stumped by this, surprisingly enough. Say: *Che ora è? Che ore sono?*

Idioms. Italian speakers do not use as many idioms as most speakers of English. Certainly, there is no flexibility, such as in English, in forming new words, and new phrases do not crop up so frequently either. English, of course, abounds in verbal idioms, of which Italian has comparatively few. Again, English contains a large number of words which each have a multiplicity of meanings (for instance, 'odd', 'bound', 'point'), of which Italian has relatively few. Idioms proper are sometimes divided into logical and non-logical, the ones whose meaning is immediately (or almost immediately) clear, and those which have to be explained to be understood. There is no hard and fast line of division between the two sorts, of course. Italian has fewer of the non-logical type than English. In short, you have no call to be so highly idiomatic in Italian as you are in English, in the sense of using idioms of the fixed sort (such as 'to beat about the bush'—in Italian, *menare il can per l'aia*). English-Italian dictionaries will often give you a description in Italian of the English expression rather than quote an Italian expression, as often there isn't one.

the rather useful plants, of which Italian has comparatively few. Again, Italian contains a large number of words which each have a multitude of meanings (for instance, I add, borrow, spend), of which Italian supplies only a few. Italian possesses just the word intellectual and senluel; the one with a ... negative is impossible for us, be-cause offensive, and the other which may ... be embodied in the mind... There is on land and fast line of division there in the ... it occurs we behold as ... or the non-Italian word in English. But only you have to call to be English the same in Italian as you are in English. In the sense of implications of the ... as you ... is, at once, at both about, the best we Italian, ... as you are ... ...

English-Italian dictionary will often give you a term in good Italian at one time that is to say, present rather than a word with Italian expression as you use here at one time.

ITALIAN-ENGLISH

A

abbigliamento (m). This is the word for the more general kind of clothes shop. Outfitters (*v.* SHOPS).

acceleratore (m). Accelerator (*v.* CARS).

accendere. To switch on the light, to switch on the engine (*accendere la luce, accendere il motore*). The opposite is *spegnere*.

accensione (f). Ignition (*v.* CARS).

accidente (m). This means 'accident' right enough, although the more usual word by far is 'incident'. *Un incidente stradale*, for example, is 'a road accident'. Another point to notice is the very similar word *accidenti* (*q.v.*).

accidenti (interj.). Italians come out with this word very frequently, mostly in just about the same situations where in English we should say 'blimey', 'struth', 'crikey' (or 'my word', 'good Lord' and so on, if you prefer); alternatively, it can be more or less 'curse it', 'blast it' and so forth. *Accidenti, che guaio!* is 'Crikey, what a mess!'

acciuga (f). Anchovy (*v.* FOOD).

accomodare. You can *accomodare* a broken tap, for example, meaning 'to fix', 'to put right' etc. Rather than 'to repair' it can mean 'to adapt' or 'to adjust'. In these senses it vies with the verb *sistemare* (*q.v.*), which is more colloquial and lower down the social scale. Then again, *accomodare* is much used reflexively, *accomodarsi* (and notice, by the way, the spelling with a single *m*). Here it means 'to take a seat', 'make yourself comfortable'. When you stand up in a bus to let someone sit down you say *Si accomodi*, or *Prego, s'accomodi*. A rather longer form is *Volete accomodarvi?* I must emphasize that this is the normal way of offering someone a seat. Don't fiddle about with the verb *sedersi* or any other verb, just say *Si accomodi*.

accordo (m). *Un accordo* is 'an agreement'. *Essere d'accordo* means 'to agree'. *D'accordo* is a very common way of indicating that 'It's all right', 'I agree'. *Sì, d'accordo, sono stato forse un po' stupido, ma adesso basta*, 'Yes, all right, I admit I've been a bit stupid, but let's have an end to it now'.

accorgersi. 'To realize', 'to notice'. Negatively, 'not to notice or realize, to be unaware of'. Take note especially of the irregular forms of this verb. *Se n'era accorto anche il capo* means 'The

19

boss had also realized it'. *Lo salutò e lui quasi non se ne accorse.* 'He greeted him almost without the other's realizing it'. *Mi sono accorto troppo tardi dell'errore,* 'Too late did I realize the mistake'. *Lo feci senza accorgermene* means 'I did it without noticing'. Another way of saying 'to realize' is *rendersi conto,* this also is much used.

accumulatore (m). Accumulator (*v.* CARS).

aceto (m). Vinegar (*v.* FOOD).

acqua (f). Water. *Acqua corrente* is 'running water', *acqua di mare* is 'sea water', *acqua di rubinetto,* 'tap water', *acqua dolce,* 'fresh water', *acqua minerale,* 'mineral water', *acqua ossigenata,* 'hydrogen peroxide', *acqua piovana,* 'rain water', *acqua potabile,* 'drinking water', *acqua ragia,* 'turpentine'.

addosso. You will come across this word in a number of expressions. For example, *avere qualcuno addosso* means 'to be stuck with someone'. *Mettere le mani addosso a qualcuno* is 'to catch hold of someone'. *Come mai posso lavorare con quel tizio addosso?* 'How on earth can I be expected to work with that fellow around?'

affare (m). This means 'a successful business deal', 'a bargain'. In various contexts it means 'business' in its different applications. Notice the expression *Si faccia gli affari suoi!* 'Mind your own business!' *Un affarone* is 'a real bargain', 'a very profitable bit of business'.

affatto. As is the case with *mica* (*q.v.*), *affatto* is used to back up and strengthen a negative. *Questo lavoro non è affatto difficile* is 'This work isn't at all hard'. *Niente affatto* means 'not at all'. *Lei dice che lui è molto simpatico, ma io non lo trovo affatto simpatico,* 'You say that he's very pleasant, but I don't find him the least bit pleasant'.

affittare. *Affittare un appartamento* is 'to rent a flat'. Stuck on the wall outside the house or flat to let you will find a red, green or yellow notice (the colours being of the luminous variety which catch the eye so readily), on which you will read *Affittasi.* The money you pay for renting a place is called *l'affitto* or else *la pigione* (*q.v.*).

affumicato. 'Smoked' (*v.* FOOD).

aglio (m). Garlic (*v.* FOOD).

agnello (m). Lamb (*v.* FOOD).

ago (m). Needle (*v.* HOUSE). *Un ago da calza* is 'a knitting needle'.

ala (f). 'Wing' in the ways the word is used in English, *viz.* of a bird, of an aeroplane, of a building and so on. In football, *l'ala destra* is 'the right winger' (*v.* SPORT).

albergo (m). Hotel (*v.* SHOPS).

albero (m). This is, of course, the word for a 'tree'. If you are learning Italian after having already studied Spanish, you will very likely have some difficulty in remembering which way round the *l* and the *r* go, as the Spanish is *arbol* and the Italian *albero*. In the section on CARS you will see that *l'albero di distribuzione* is 'the camshaft' and the *albero a manovella* is the 'crankshaft'.

albicocca (f). Apricot (*v.* FOOD).

allenare. To train. 'Training' is *allenamento* and the 'trainer' is *l'allenatore*. Note that the *allenatore* is a very important personage in Italian sporting life, and that the important teams of the First Division (*Serie A*) spend large amounts of money on obtaining an efficient trainer. You may train out on the field, *campo*, or again inside in the gymnasium, *la palestra*.

allora. You know that this means 'then', as opposed to 'now', which is *adesso*. (Spanish speakers, note that it is easy to confuse *ahora* and *allora*.) Apart from this time meaning, *allora* is used, and used again and again, more or less in the same way as *dunque* (*q.v.*), meaning 'well', or perhaps more with the idea of 'well, then'. There are countless situations where this word can be used. A lady goes into a shop where she has already left an order. Looking at the assistant, she says: *Allora, è tutto pronto?* On a crowded bus, a young lady is standing beside a young man, whose hand inadvertently touches hers on the rail they are both holding for support. Suspecting that the poor chap is getting a bit fresh, the young lady fixes him with a glare and exclaims: *Allora?* 'Well, what d'you think you're up to?' Another example: the teacher has set an exercise, and gives the class a certain time to do it in. When the time is up, he says: *Allora, non scrivete più,* 'Now then, don't write any more'. Just one more: some friends have had a bit of a discussion about where to go that evening. After examining each other's suggestions, they say: *Allora, dove andiamo?* 'Well now, where are we going?' *Allora, ha capito?*

ammortizzatore (m). Shock-absorber (*v.* CARS).

Anagrafe (f). *L'Ufficio dell'Anagrafe*, or simply *l'Anagrafe*, is where you have to go to register births, deaths, marriages, residence and so on. The Registry Office, in other words.

ananasso (m). Pineapple (*v.* FOOD).

ancora. Here I am referring to the word with the accent on the middle syllable, and not to the noun of the same spelling which takes the accent on the first syllable (i.e. *l'ancora*, 'the anchor'). You will be aware of the different meanings of this word. Firstly, we have 'yet' and 'still'. *Non sono ancora arrivati* means 'They are not yet here'. *Mio fratello era ancora in casa quando io sono uscito* is 'My brother was still at home when I left'. Secondly, *ancora* can mean 'even' in the sense of 'still', together with a comparative. 'And her sister is even prettier' would be, for example, *E sua sorella è ancora più carina*. *Ancora meglio* is 'even better'. Thirdly, we have the idea of 'more'. *Ne vuoi ancora?* is 'Do you want some more?' *Ancora cinque, per favore*, is 'Five more, please'. *Ancora un po'* means 'Just a little more'. And fourthly, there is the idea of repetition, of 'again'. For instance, *L'ho visto ancora una volta stamane* means 'I saw him once again this morning'.

andare. This is one of the key verbs of the Italian vocabulary. Of course, it is heard most often in the form *va*. *Come va?* means 'How are things going?' and so on. *Va bene* is equivalent to our 'All right' or 'O.K.'. *Me ne vado* means 'I'm going', from the verb *andarsene*. *Vado a vedere un film* means 'I'm going to see a film', although you should be a bit careful not to overwork the construction *andare a fare qualche cosa*, which is not of such frequent occurrence as the 'I'm going to' construction in English. At night you *va a letto*, 'go to bed'. *Andare a piedi* is 'to go on foot', while *andare in bicicletta* is 'to cycle'. *Le cose vanno avanti molto bene* means 'Things are going on very nicely, thank you'. Notice especially the form *andiamo*, the Italian equivalent of the French '*on y va*' and the Spanish '*vamos*', not to mention the English 'let's go', 'come on'. From this we have the noun *andata* (f), of special use to train users. *Un biglietto di andata e ritorno* is 'a return ticket', as opposed to 'a single', which is *un biglietto di sola andata*.

anitra (f). Duck (*v.* FOOD). Accent on first syllable.

antichità (f). This is the word written on shops which sell antiques (*v.* SHOPS).

antipasto (m). *Pasto* is 'meal', and what is eaten before the meal (?) is the 'hors d'œuvres'. The reason for the question mark is the size of some people's *antipasto*, making it hardly possible to say that this is something prior to and separate from the main meal.

anzi. Usually this means 'or rather', used in the following manner: *Probabilmente lo faranno. Anzi, sicuramente*, 'They'll probably do it, or rather they're sure to'. *Questa sera fa caldo. Anzi, si scoppia*, 'It's hot this evening, or rather it's scorching'. *È una ragazza molto intelligente. Anzi, è un genio*, 'She's a very intelligent girl, or rather she's a genius'. You will of course have noticed how in Italian there is a full stop and a new sentence, while in English we usually have a comma.

aperitivo (m). Aperitif (*v.* FOOD).

apparecchio (m). This refers to all sorts of apparatus, but its special application is to the telephone.

appuntare. Do not think that this has anything to do with appointing. 'To appoint' is *nominare*, as often as not, while *appuntare* is 'to sharpen'.

appunto (m). As a noun, this means 'note'. 'To take notes' is normally *prendere appunti*. (Get used to this expression, and don't let yourself say *prendere una nota* if you can help it. Italians do say *prendere delle note*, but *appunti* is colloquial.) Now, the important point here is the use of *appunto* as an adverb, meaning 'just', 'precisely' and so on. *Sono venuto appunto perchè . . .* means 'I've come precisely because . . . '. *Appunto per questo l'ho detto*, 'That's just why I said it'. *Lei deve pagare.—Sì, appunto per questo sono venuto*, 'You have to pay.'—'Yes, that's the very reason why I've come'. You frequently hear the single word *appunto* as a comment referring to someone else's statement. This shows that the speaker is putting in a 'that's right' or a 'precisely', in agreement.

aragosta (f). Lobster (*v.* FOOD).

arancia (f). Orange (*v.* FOOD). *Una spremuta d'arancia* is 'a drink of orange squash'.

arbitro (m). Referee (*v.* SPORT). There's no playing about in Italian with different words for different sports, as in English (*e.g.* 'referee' for boxing and football, 'umpire' for tennis and cricket). No, there's just plain *arbitro*.

archiviare. 'To file', that's to say 'to put away in a file'. The word for the tool of the same name is *una lima*, while 'file' in the sense of a long line of people is plain *fila*. *L'archivio* refers to 'the files', whereas a 'file' meaning some sort of cover in which to file the correspondence on a certain subject would be *pratica* (f). A *raccoglitore* (m) is a stiff-backed cover in which you keep papers, usually in a stiff clip or with punched holes.

argomento (m). This is not an argument in the English sense of something to shout at somebody about, bang your fist on the table, or perhaps even go further in the process of getting your point across or defending your view. The Italian *argomento* is more 'the topic of conversation', 'the subject being discussed'. *Seguire l'argomento* is 'to follow the conversation'. The English 'argument' would be more *discussione* (f), or perhaps *una disputa*, this being more 'quarrel'. *Luigi ha avuto una disputa con sua moglie riguardante un argomento che ora non ricordo* can be 'Luigi had an argument with his wife about some subject I can't remember now'. 'To argue' may be *ragionare, discutere* or *avere una disputa*, according to the context or the tone of the argument. In the sense of 'reason', *e.g.* 'you have a good argument there', say *ragionamento* or perhaps here *argomento*. An ordinary talk to someone, by the way, is a *colloquio* or a *discorso*, although these words may sound too elegant to the English ear. 'A chat' is *una chiacchierata*.

aria (f). Air in general, as in English, as in 'fresh air', 'she has a superior air about her', 'to put on airs' and so on. In a car *l'aria* refers to 'the choke'. Many Italians, by the way, ascribe small upsets, illnesses, etc., to *un colpo d'aria*, 'a draught'.

aringa (f). Herring (*v.* FOOD).

arredamenti (m pl). House equipment. The word often put outside shops selling furniture (*mobili*, m pl).

arrivare. This presents little difficulty, really, if you realize that when we say 'to get there' in English, we could usually say 'to arrive' just as correctly, which means in fact that Italians appear to be over-using their word *arrivare* to our ears. *Arrivare con un ritardo di 5 minuti* means 'to arrive 5 minutes late'. A useful expression is *Non ci arrivo*, literally 'I don't arrive there', meaning also 'It's beyond me', 'I can't understand it'. The noun corresponding to *arrivare* is *arrivo* (m), 'arrival'. *Essere in arrivo* is 'to be arriving, to be just coming in'.

arrosto (m). Roast (*v.* FOOD). Roast meat can be either *carne arrostita* from the verb *arrostire*, or *arrosto di carne*, the latter being the more usual. *Arrostire sulla graticola* is 'to grill'. *Arrosto alla griglia* is 'a grill'.

asparago (m). Asparagus (*v.* FOOD).

aspirapolvere (m). Vacuum cleaner (*v.* HOUSEHOLD). The verb *aspirare* may be 'to aspire', 'to aspirate' or 'to inhale, breathe in'. The Italian vacuum cleaner, as you can see, 'inhales dust'.

assale (m). Axle (*v.* CARS).

assegno (m). Cheque (*v.* OFFICE).

assistere. Something of a false friend, although not so much so in Italian as in some languages. To help is normally *aiutare*, but *assistere* can be used sometimes. On the other hand, *assistere* more often means 'to attend, be present at'.

atleta (m). Athlete (*v.* SPORT).

atletica (f). Athletics (*v.* SPORT).

attaccare. This can be an 'unreliable friend' at times. Admittedly, it does mean 'to attack', which can also be *assalire*. But the normal meaning of the verb is 'to stick, fasten' and so on. *Vado a attaccare i francobolli, poi a imbucare le lettere* means 'I'm going to stick the stamps on and then post the letters'. Using a piece of string or rope the verb indicates 'to tie'. Reflexively, the verb usually indicates 'to stick to'. In sport, *l'attacco* is 'the attack', or perhaps 'the forward line', while *un attaccante* is one of these, 'a forward'.

attendere. This is not 'to attend', which is *assistere*, but rather 'to wait', which makes it sound somewhat archaic to us. Telling someone to wait a moment, you can use this verb, *attenda un momento*, or else the verb *aspettare*, which is certainly more common in normal everyday conversation. You will hear fifty times *aspetti* for every once you hear *attenda*. *Aspetti un attimo* means 'Hang on just half a tick'.

attenzione. This is the usual warning to 'be careful'. You can also put it this way: *Stia attento*, 'Look out'. *Stare attento* is used a good deal, in fact. *La polizia deve stare attenta a tutto* means 'The police have to be on the lookout for everything'.

atterrare. To knock down. Used in boxing, where a boxer (*un pugile*) may *atterrare* his opponent (*avversario*), with a right hook (*gancio destro*) for example.

attico (m). If you search the advertisement columns of the Italian papers, hoping to find a suitable flat, you will think it rather strange that they ask more for an 'attic' than for a luxurious apartment—until you realize that *attico* is another of our famous 'false friends' and means 'penthouse'. Now, I must say that 'penthouse' doesn't sound so attractive to English ears as *attico* does to Italian ears. We just don't go in for them. But many Italians highly appreciate the advantages they offer —a terrace at the top of the building, to take the sun while at the same time getting the benefits of the breezes, with a fine view of the town too, very likely. For reference, the English word 'attic' can best be translated into Italian as *soffitta*— and don't say *soffitto*, which of course means 'ceiling'.

attirare. Another false friend, but one you are probably aware of. It means 'to attract', while 'attire', as in 'his attire', is usually *vestiti* (m pl), 'clothes'.

attualmente. Another false friend, not meaning 'actually', which can be variously *realmente*, *dunque*, *infatti* and so on, but 'at present', 'now'. *Attuale* means 'present' or 'topical'. *Attualità* are 'things of interest at the present time' or 'topical matters'.

augurio (m). A good wish. This is a very often-used word, almost always in the plural *auguri*. It is the stock word for wishing 'good luck' and 'best wishes', ousting all other words. You'd use it to wish good luck to someone about to take his finals (*fare gli esami*), someone embarking on a journey (*buon viaggio ed auguri*), someone about to get married and so on. And not just when people are *about* to do something, as it is used also to give good wishes on birthdays, saints' days (*onomastici*) and other occasions. *Il primo contatto con loro è stato di buon augurio*. This is an example of the use of the singular form, and means 'The first contact with them has been promising (of good omen)'.

The verb is *augurare*, meaning either 'to portend', 'to promise', or 'to wish', in this way—*Vi auguro buon viaggio*, 'I wish you a pleasant journey'.

autista (m). Chauffeur. Driver is normally *conducente*, from the verb *condurre*.

autonoleggio (m). Car-hire (*v.* CARS).

autorimessa (f). Most languages use the word 'garage', and this is certainly to be encountered also in Italian. But signs outside garages will normally advertise *autorimessa*.

avanti. When someone knocks on the office door, the call to tell him to enter is this, *Avanti*, 'forward'. Here, therefore, it means 'Come in'. Apart from this, the word is obviously one of those that you will constantly be having to use. *Non possiamo andare avanti così* means 'We can't go on like this'. *D'ora in avanti* is 'from now on'. In urging someone to go forward, to go on, to do something, you would encourage him by saying *Avanti*. *Più avanti* is 'further on'.

avversario (m). Opponent (*v.* SPORT).

avvisatore (m) **acustico.** An acoustic signal-call apparatus or, less poetically, the 'hooter' of a car (*v.* CARS).

azzurro (m). Most foreign visitors to Britain, or foreign readers of our sports news, are initially mystified by references to 'He is a triple blue', and so on—but perhaps Italians are less puzzled than others, as they themselves use the word in sport. Their use is different from the English meaning of 'representative of the university', however, as in Italian it means 'a representative of Italy', otherwise called *un nazionale* (as opposed to the English term 'international'). *Gli azzurri* is often written instead of 'Italy' or 'our team'.

B

bagnato. I put this in simply because I have so often heard learners struggling to find the simple word 'wet'. *Sono arrivato a casa tutto bagnato* means 'I arrived home completely soaked'.

bagno (m). Bath, bathroom (*v.* HOUSEHOLD).

ballo (m). Yes, the ordinary word for 'dance'. The verb is *ballare*. Sounds a bit highfalutin to the English ear, perhaps, to refer to any old dance as a *ballo*, but there it is. The word can also give the idea of 'to be a question of' or 'to be at stake'. *Questa persona non era in ballo* means 'There was no mention of this person'. *Il mio onore è in ballo* is 'My honour is at stake'.

banca (f), **banco** (m). Bank, where you put your money. One of those few words which can be used with either a feminine or a masculine ending. You find, for example, the *Banco di*

Roma and the *Banco di Santo Spirito*, as against the *Banca Nazionale Del Lavoro* and the *Banca d'America e d'Italia*. The plural is normally *banche*. Another word for a bank, in the name of the bank at any rate, is *credito*. There are, for instance, the *Credito Italiano* and the *Credito di Venezia e del Rio de la Plata*.

bar (m). Italy is full of small bars, where you may have your drink of tea or coffee (usually coffee), of fruit squash (*spremuta di limone*, etc.), of beer, of liqueur or anything else. If you are thinking in terms of the bar of a public-house, where you go for a glass of beer, then try a *birreria*, where you may also eat sausages, goulash and so on. But you will not find many such places.

barattolo (m). Tin or pot (*v.* HOUSEHOLD).

barbabietola (f). Beetroot (*v.* FOOD).

battere. To beat (*v.* SPORT). *Battere a macchina* is 'to type' (*v.* OFFICE).

batteria (f). Battery, such as the one in a car, but also, in sport, 'heat'. *Ha vinto la prima batteria*, 'He has won the first heat'.

battistrada (f). Tread of a tyre (*v.* CARS).

Befana (f). According to the calendar, this is Epiphany. According to Italian children, *la Befana* is 'the Twelfth Night Witch', armed with a broomstick, and associated with the giving of presents. Present-day custom tends more and more towards giving presents at Christmas, but Italians being so enamoured of buying large and expensive presents for children, *regali della Befana* are not dying out. In Rome, for instance, the place to visit at Befana is the Piazza Navona, where numerous stalls stand loaded with large and small gifts for children.

bello. This means 'beautiful', and you should already be able to manipulate it very well. Just note two things. *Bella* is perhaps the only common Italian *piropo* or compliment passed in the street when a man sees a girl or a lady go past. And certainly you will hear it addressed much more to children than to adults. People turn in the street to look at a child who is beautiful, gay, eye-catching in some way or other, and they will say *bello* or, more usually, *bella*. The second thing to note is the expression *fare una bella figura* (opposite, *fare una brutta figura*). This is all a question of appearances, of social prestige, of face. You do not perhaps want to do something, to say something, to give something, to offer something, but you are forced to do so for the sake of 'what people would think'. If you did not do it, you would be making *una brutta figura*. 'It's only a small firm (*ditta*), but they have magnificent notepaper'—just to *fare una bella figura*, naturally!

bene. I certainly don't intend to go through all the possible uses of this word, most of which you should be conversant with at all events. Suffice to note some of the most-used expressions, not always to be found in the dictionary, let alone given any stress. *Va bene* means 'All right' or 'O.K.', and *Va bene così?* is 'Is it all right like this?' *Non suona bene* shows that 'It doesn't sound right'. *Speriamo bene* means 'Let's hope it turns out all right', 'Let's hope for the best'. *Due signori molto per bene* are 'two gentlemen, real gentlemen', referring to their gentlemanly characters, or perhaps to their social standing. *Ti sta bene* means 'Serves you right'. *Comportarsi bene* is 'to behave well'. The variations of *bene* are *benissimo*, very frequently heard, *benino* and *benone*. *Benino* is 'quite well', 'pretty well', and *benone* means 'very well', 'very well indeed'. *Benissimo* means 'excellent', 'excellently', 'very good' etc., and it is used by teachers, for example, when a correct answer is given by the student, and in many other circumstances to give praise. You might also often hear the short *be'*. In fact, certain people seem hardly to be able to begin a sentence without first saying *be'*. 'And how did you find the people there?' (*E come ha trovato la gente lì?*)—*Be', Be', non so, ho trovato la gente molto simpatica, insomma* ('Well, I don't know, I found the people very pleasant on the whole').

benzina (f). Petrol (*v.* CARS). The Italian *petrolio* corresponds to the English 'oil', and also to 'kerosene' or 'coal oil'. *Trovare il petrolio* is the unlikely but true rendering of 'to strike oil'.

bere. To drink. A drink is *una bibita* or *una bevanda* (*v.* FOOD).

bicchiere (m). The glass you drink out of, or 'tumbler'. Don't, whatever you do, confuse it with the glass you look through, which you must be aware is *vetro*. Again, the glass you look into, or rather mirror, is *uno specchio*.

bidè (m). We have to be satisfied with the French word in English, *bidet*. In France and in Italy, the *bidet* is a normal household fixture, although a rarity in an English house. The word is therefore more important than it might seem to the person who is not aware of conditions in Italy.

bidone (m). A *bidone* is a 'container', a 'can'. People often associate it with petrol, therefore a 'jerry-can'. And a full jerry-can is heavy, and as with *mattone* (*q.v.*) the idea of heaviness is transferred figuratively, making the thing it is applied to 'boring'. The most exact rendering of *un bidone*, to describe a dance, or a play, or a new girl friend, or something else of which you had greater hopes or expectations, is 'a dead loss'. *Bidonata* (f) is a variation of *bidone*.

biella (f). Connecting rod (*v.* CARS).

birra (f). Beer. To be bought in a 'bar' or, if you do not wish to have the bottled variety, in a *birreria* (f), which can be called a 'beer garden' or 'alehouse' or 'beer restaurant'.

biscotti (m pl). Biscuits (*v.* FOOD).

bisognare. 'Must' and so forth, as you will be well aware. You may either use it simply, followed by an infinitive, or with *che*, followed by a subjunctive. *Per ottenere un grosso successo bisognerà allenare molto*, 'To obtain any real success, a lot of training will be necessary'. *Non bisogna dimenticare che è molto lontano*, 'It mustn't be forgotten that it's very far away'. *Bisogna che lui vada via*, 'He must go away'. *Non bisogna esagerare* is 'Now, don't exaggerate'. *See also* the notes on *ci vuole* under **volere**.

bisogno (m). 'Need'. *Ho bisogno di sonno* means 'I need some sleep'. *Quella ragazza non ha bisogno di nulla* is 'That girl has everything she wants'. *Ne ho bisogno* is 'I need it'. *Chi va in treno non ha bisogno di risolvere il problema della strada* means 'Those who go by train have no call to face up to the road problem'. The most important thing to note is the use of *Non c'è bisogno di . . .*, 'There's no need to . . .'. For instance, *Non c'è bisogno di dire niente*, 'There's no need to say anything'.

bistecca (f). Beef steak (*v.* FOOD).

blocco (m) **cilindri**. Cylinder block (*v.* CARS).

bobina (f). Spool, reel or coil. In a car, it is the 'coil' (*v.* CARS).

bollitore (m). Kettle (*v.* HOUSEHOLD). *Un bollitore elettrico* is, of course, 'an electric kettle'.

bombola (f) **di gas.** A gas container. It is quite a common system in Italy to have these gas containers delivered to the house, to provide the gas for the cooker and a gas-fire, perhaps.

borsa (f). This can be a 'bag', a 'purse' and so on. Students may have the good fortune to obtain a *borsa di studio*, a 'scholarship'. The *Borsa Valori* is the 'Stock Exchange', while the *borsa nera* is the 'black market'. In sport, especially in boxing, *la borsa* is 'the purse'.

bottega (f). Shop (*v.* SHOPS). A more usual word is *negozio* (m). The word *ditta* is best translated 'firm'. *Un magazzino* is usually 'a store'.

bottiglia (f). Bottle (*v.* HOUSEHOLD). *Un cavatappi* is the word for 'a corkscrew'.

bracciolo (m). Arm-rest (*v.* CARS).

braciola (f). Chop or cutlet (*v.* FOOD). The word you will probably come across most frequently for this is, however, *cotoletta*.

bravo. A false friend. *È molto bravo* refers, not to his courage, but to his ability, meaning 'He is very clever'. *Bravo* gives this idea of 'clever' or 'good'. The English 'brave' is best rendered as *coraggioso*.

briciola (f). Crumb (*v.* FOOD).

brillo. This adjective is one of the many, Italian being no different from other languages in this respect, to give the idea of being somewhat sozzled. *Era un po' brillo sabato sera* means 'He was a bit tight on Saturday evening'.

brodo (m). Soup. Broth type (*v*. FOOD).

bucato (m). The washing, the week's wash, the laundry. You can see this word everywhere in advertisements for soap powders. *È facile fare il bucato con il nuovo XX—e che bel bucato bianco e veramente pulito*, 'It's simple to do the wash with the new XX—and what beautiful washing, white and really clean'.

bucatura (f). Puncture. *See also* **puntura**.

budino (m). Pudding—but don't expect any word to translate pudding exactly, in all its varieties. *Dolce* is another word quite often used for puddings of the sweet variety.

buffo. Ridiculous, silly, comical. *Forse sembra un po' buffo, ma è infatti successo così*, 'Perhaps you'll think it's a bit ridiculous, but that's the way it really happened'. *Mi trovo in una situazione molto buffa* is 'I am in a very stupid predicament'.

bugia (f). This corresponds to 'lie', 'nonsense' and 'rubbish'. Most often used in the plural, *dire bugie*. The word *Bugie* used in replying to someone is about the same as saying 'Rubbish', 'I don't believe a word of it'. *Un bugiardo* is one who tells lies, 'a liar'.

buio (m). This is both noun and adjective, and I remind you of it as so many people neglect it altogether and look for another word, such as *oscuro*, to mean 'dark'. Of course, *oscuro* does mean 'dark', but *buio* has a wide meaning, extending from the dark of night and unlit rooms to the darkness of not knowing what's going on. Thus: *È buio* means just 'It's dark'. *Questa è la sala da pranzo; è buio, ma tanto ci si vede abbastanza*, 'This is the dining-room; it's dark, but still you can see quite enough of it'. On the other hand, *È completamente al buio di questa faccenda* means 'He's completely in the dark about this business'.

burro (m). Spanish speakers beware. This is the classical Spanish—Italian false friend, meaning 'butter' in Italian (as opposed to 'donkey' in Spanish).

busta (f). Envelope (*v*. OFFICE). *Una busta a finestra* is 'a window envelope', while a *busta paga* is a 'pay envelope'. And mind you don't say *busto* instead of *busta*.

buttare. This means 'to throw'. *Buttare via* is 'to throw away'. 'To throw' can also be *lanciare*, but this gives more an idea of precision, and is in fact the word used in those sports where something is thrown. For example, *lanciare il giavellotto* is 'to throw the javelin'. Note also the idiomatic use of *buttare via* and *buttare giù*. (And another thing to note is the common dropping of the final *e* of the infinitive in such phrasal verbs as *buttar via* and *buttar giù*.) When you say of something that *non è da buttar via*, you convey the impression that it's worthwhile, that you wouldn't cast it aside. *Buttar giù* is literally 'to fling down'. Here I must quote two friends of mine. One of them is a publicity agent and is always making notes of ideas and phrases as they occur to him—or, as he puts it, he is always having to *buttar giù* something on paper. The other friend was recently waiting, with his wife and myself, for another guest to arrive. After half an hour, he said to his wife that she had better *buttar giù* the meat to grill, as he was *stufo* (or 'fed up') with waiting.

C

cacciavite (m). Screwdriver (*v.* CARS). Tools for general use are *attrezzatura generica*, while an *utensile* is a tool in the mechanical sense. A screw is *una vite*.

caffè (m). Coffee. You go into a *bar* (often advertised as a *bar-gelateria* or *bar-caffè* or *pasticceria*), order your drink, pay and receive a ticket, which you present to the *barista* behind another counter together with a ten-lire tip (per person), telling him what you have already paid for. The system is a little complicated. Regarding what sort of coffee you want, *caffè con latte* is '*café au lait*', *cappuccino* is similar but with less milk and less in quantity, a *caffè lungo* (just say *un lungo*) is ordinary black coffee with a few more drops of water than the ordinary *espresso*. If you want your coffee even stronger than the normal (and quite strong) *espresso*, ask for *caffè ristretto*, but this is somewhat unusual. Then you might like something in your coffee, perhaps? Laced with a drop of spirits, usually anisette or brandy, it is referred to as *caffè corretto*. Just one more variation—you will see some people taking their coffee with just a wee spot of milk in it, hardly enough to make any difference, you'd think. This is called a *caffè macchiato*. A coffee-pot is *una caffettiera*.

calciatore (m). Footballer (*v.* SPORT).

calcio (m). This is the national sport of football. *Un calcio* also means 'a kick'. *Tirare* is the verb most often heard meaning 'to shoot'. *Un calcio d'angolo* is 'a corner kick', *un calcio di punizione* is 'a free kick', and *un calcio di rigore* is 'a penalty'.

calcolatrice (f). This piece of office equipment is a 'computer'.

calzolaio (m). Shoemaker. The shop will probably have this word outside. Shoes are of course *scarpe* (f). *Calzature* (f) is 'footwear'.

cambiare. To change. The verb also includes changing money, for example, and *cambio* (m) is the word for 'rate of exchange'.

camera (f). Of course you realize that this is a 'room' and not a 'camera'. There are many words which can be added to modify the meaning. For example, *camera d'aria* is an 'inner tube'; *camera di commercio* is 'chamber of commerce'; *camera oscura* is a 'darkroom' and so on.

camiceria (f). Shirt shop (*v.* SHOPS).

campare. Dictionary-wise, this is 'to live'. But of course you don't *campare* in Via Eleonora Duse, for example (*abitare*). *Campare* is more in keeping with *vivere*, and the following gives a good indication of its usage: *Uno lavora, ma a che scopo? Per campare? Si può campare anche senza ammazzarsi dal lavoro* ('You work, but for what purpose? To live? You can live just as well without killing yourself with work').

campionato (m). Championship (*v.* SPORT). When a fight is for a title, it is common to say that it is *valevole per il titolo europeo*, for instance.

campione (m). Champion (*v.* SPORT).

campo (m). Field. *Campo di gioco* is 'playing-field'. 'Ground' and 'pitch' are other possible translations. *Campo del tiro a segno* is a 'rifle-range'. *Campo di battaglia* is a 'battleground'. *Campo di visibilità* is the 'range of visibility'. *Campo magnetico* is a 'magnetic field'.

cancellare. To rub out, erase. The English 'cancel' is usually *annullare*.

candela (f). Candle (*v.* HOUSEHOLD). Sparking plug (*v.* CARS).

cannella (f). Cinnamon (*v.* FOOD).

canottaggio (m). Rowing (*v.* SPORT).

cantina (f). The cellar of a house. This is a false friend, having no connexion with the English 'canteen', which can be variously *borraccia* and *bidone*, in the sense of a container as used in the army, or *ristorante*, in the sense of the place where you eat.

capace. *Sono capace di fare questo* means 'I'm able to do this'. *Non sono capace di capire quando lui parla*, is 'I can't understand when he speaks'. *Capace* is 'able' rather than 'capable'. It is usually easier, of course, to use the verb *potere*, but this construction, more often negative than positive, is common.

capirai. This exclamation is, as you can see, from the verb *capire*. The meaning varies from 'You can just imagine' and 'Just imagine that', to 'What the dickens'. *Capirai, mi vuole cacciare via senza spiegare niente*, 'Just imagine, he wants to give me the sack without any explanation'. It is a sign of indignation, more often than not.

capire. To understand. When telling you something, an Italian will very often put in the occasional *Ha capito?* or just plain *Capito?* and you will add your *Ho capito* or just plain *Capito*. This is more or less equivalent to the English 'D'you see?' and 'I see'. Notice the similarity to the verb *capitare* (*q.v.*), meaning 'to happen'. *Capire qualche cosa a volo* is 'to take the hint'.

capitare. To happen, which is more often *accadere*, and even more frequently *succedere*. *Mi capita a volte di . . .* is quite a common construction, meaning 'It sometimes happens that I . . .'. Note that the emphasis on this word is on the first syllable—*cApita*.

capo (m). I mention this to point out that *il capo* is 'the boss', and that *cominciare una cosa da capo* is 'to begin something from the beginning, to start again right from the very beginning'. *Il capolinea* is 'the terminal station', or 'terminus' of a bus route. Naturally *capo* is the 'head', and note that it is also the 'headland' or 'cape' in geography.

caraffa (f). Jug. It always seems difficult to find translations of simple household containers. In many languages people take hours to decide what something simple like a 'kettle' is called. Italians take their time about giving a jug a name, but it is in fact generally *una caraffa*.

caratteri (m) **bastone.** Block letters (*v.* OFFICE).

carburatore (m). Carburettor (*v.* CARS).

carciofo (m). Artichoke (*v.* FOOD).

cardine (m). Hinge (*v.* HOUSEHOLD).

carino. This corresponds pretty much to the English adjective 'pretty'. (Note that it absolutely cannot be the English adverb 'pretty', as used in the first line here, which is usually *abbastanza* or *pressappoco*.) The Italian *carino* also refers sometimes to something not necessarily pretty, but 'nice'. However, *carino* is not done to death to anything like the extent the English 'nice' is. Italian also has *simpatico*, as well as *buono*, *bello*, *grazioso* and *piacevole*, according to context. *Carino* usually gives the idea of prettiness, however, of something sweet. My youngest daughter, aged five, being blonde and full of life, often causes people to remark *Che carina!* Now, she also happens to be called Karina. Hence the usual small-talk conversation in buses, shops etc. *Come si chiama la bambina?—Si chiama Karina.—Sì, d'accordo, è molto carina, ma come si chiama?* And so on.

carità (f). Charity. Notice the expression *per carità*, which gives the same impression, approximately, as 'for Heaven's sake!'

carne (f). Meat. *Carne in scatola* is 'tinned meat'. *Un chilo di carne macinata* is 'a kilo of ground meat'.

carota (f). Carrot (*v.* FOOD).

carta (f). Paper (but never a newspaper, which is *un giornale*).
Here is a list (*elenco*) of some of the more important sorts of
paper:

> *carta asciugante*, blotting paper
> *carta carbone*, carbon paper
> *carta da bollo*, stamped paper, official paper
> *carta da imballaggio*, packing paper
> *carta da scrivere*, writing paper
> *carta igienica*, toilet paper
> *carta intestata*, letter head
> *carta per ciclostile*, duplicating paper
> *carta protocollo*, foolscap paper
> *carta straccia*, waste paper

Another way of saying *carta da bollo* is *carta bollata*, and this
sort of paper is very much in use, as it is prescribed by official
bodies when you make a request for a work permit (*permesso
di lavoro*) and so on.

carter (m). Crankcase (*v.* CARS).

cartoleria (f). Stationer's (*v.* SHOPS).

cartolina (f) **postale**. Post card (*v.* OFFICE).

casalinghi. From the adjective *casalingo*, meaning 'domestic'.
This word can be read on shops offering domestic require-
ments for sale. Household articles, or perhaps 'ironmongery'.

cascare. To fall, and a very common verb. *Casco dalla fame* is
'I'm dying of hunger'.

caso (m). 'Case', in most cases. *In caso di bisogno* is 'in case of
necessity'. *In tale caso* means 'that being the case', 'in that
case'. *Il caso è che . . .* means 'the point is that . . .'. *Lui ne
prese uno a caso* is 'He took one of them at random'. *Con
me, non è il caso che tu ti senta a disagio*, 'With me you don't
have to feel uneasy'. *Non ci ho fatto caso* means 'I didn't
notice it'. Note especially the expression *caso mai* (*v.* **mai**),
meaning 'just in case'. Two more things. Firstly, the expression *nel mio caso*, meaning 'in my case'; and secondly, *un
caso di forza maggiore*, which is clearly 'a case of something
beyond control'. In my experience, this expression is over-
worked as an excuse, including many things which could
quite easily have been avoided. *Come vedete, è un caso di forza
maggiore*, 'As you can see, it's completely beyond my control'.
Well, often it isn't, or wasn't.

cassa (f). Box (*v.* HOUSEHOLD) and Cash desk (*v.* OFFICE).

cassaforte (f). Literally, 'strongbox', which it is, a 'safe' (*v.*
OFFICE).

casseruola (f). Here you will recognize the word 'casserole', and
it does in fact mean 'saucepan' (*v.* HOUSEHOLD).

cassetto (m). Drawer (of a desk, for example) (*v.* OFFICE).

cassiere (m). Cashier (*v.* OFFICE).

catena (f). Chain. In the north of Italy it is sometimes necessary to use 'skid chains' in the winter, and these are *catene anti-sdrucciolevoli* or *catene da neve*. *Una catena di montagne* is 'a range of mountains'. *Reazione a catena* is 'chain reaction'.

cavalli (m pl). *Cavallo* is of course 'horse', and the plural is commonly used to mean 'horse-power'. The singular is also used in this way—'a horse-power of . . . ', *cavallo di. . . .*

cavare. Passing by some of the dictionary definitions, we come to the word 'get'. Now *cavare* is nothing like so comprehensive as our famous 'get', but corresponds in a number of ways. The paper tells us that so-and-so has had an accident, but that *se la caverà* ('he'll pull through, get better again'). *Cavare soldi allo zio* is 'to get money out of uncle'. If you can't get the hang of something, you may say that *non riesco a cavarne nulla*. If someone is in a fix, we hope that he'll *cavarsela*, 'get out of it'. Note also that *cavare* means 'satisfy', in the sense of satisfying hunger, thirst, wish etc.(*cavarsi la fame, la sete, la voglia di fare qualcosa* etc.).

cavolfiore (m). Cauliflower (*v.* FOOD).

cavolini (m pl). Sprouts (*v.* FOOD). If you wish to specify the place, you may add *di Bruxelles*.

cavolo (m). Cabbage (*v.* FOOD).

cena (f). The evening meal, that is, supper or dinner. '*La Cena di Leonardo*' is the way Italians refer to what we call 'The Last Supper'.

centralino (m). This is the telephone exchange. You may also call it *la centrale telefonica*. *Centrale interurbana* is 'trunk exchange'.

centravanti (m). Centre-forward (*v.* SPORT).

centro mediano (m). Centre-half (*v.* SPORT).

certo. 'Surely', in the sense of 'certainly', 'of course'. *Posso chiedere un favore?—Certo* ('May I ask a favour?' 'Yes, of course').

cestino (m). Basket, waste paper basket (*v.* OFFICE).

chiacchiere(f pl)Chatter, gossip (a *chiacchierone* is a 'chatterbox'). Multiply this word four times, and it becomes a much-used expression: *fare quattro chiacchiere con qualcuno* is 'to have a chat with someone'. *Vado là a fare quattro chiacchiere* means 'I'm going there to have a bit of a chat'.

chiacchierare. To chatter or gossip. 'To gossip' may also be *ciarlare.*

chiasso (m). Noise, din, row, racket. For example: *Faceva il più chiasso possibile per non sentire il rumore della strada*, 'She made as much row as she could so as not to hear the sounds from the street'.

chiave (f). Key. Also a 'spanner'. *Una chiave dell'accensione* is 'an ignition key'. *Chiave fissa doppia* is 'double-ended spanner'. The best-known one of all is the *chiave inglese*, which is a 'monkey wrench'.

chiodo (m). Nail, which you hit with a hammer (*martello*). The nails on your fingers are your *unghie* (f pl).

ci. Your elementary studies will have shown you the varied meanings of *ci*. There are the following: here; there (place); there (with verb 'to be'); it; us, ourselves, each other, one another. It is imperative to be fully conversant with these various applications of the word if you are to speak the language well. *C'è* means 'There is' and also the question form 'Is there?' What's more, when asking whether someone is at home, on the telephone or in person, you say *C'è Massimo?* for example. *Ce ne sono* means 'There are some (of them)'. *Ci sto molto bene* means 'I'm doing very well here', 'I'm getting on mighty fine here'. *Ci siamo* may be 'Here we are', while as a question *Ci siamo?* it asks 'Are we agreed, then?', apart from 'Are we there?' *Non ce l'ho* means 'I haven't got it'. *Ci vediamo*, literally 'We see each other', gives the same idea as 'I'll be seeing you' or, as in *Ci vediamo spesso durante l'estate*, 'We often meet during the summer'. *Ci penso io* promises 'I'll take care of that', 'Leave that to me', 'I'll deal with that, don't you worry'. *Ci manderanno i soldi fra poco* means 'They'll be sending us the cash before long'. If someone advises you that he doesn't believe something, he may say *Non ci credo*, 'I don't believe it'. *Ci provi* means 'Have a go at it', 'Try' and so on. *Che c'entra Massimo in tutto ciò?—Osvaldo, sì, c'entra.* 'Where does Massimo come into all this?'—'Osvaldo comes into it, though'.

For *ci vuole* ('is needed') *see* **volere**. Lastly, note the expression *C'è da fare una cosa*, meaning 'Something has to be done'. *C'è da pagare mille lire* is 'There's 1000 lire to pay'.

ciao. 'Cheerio'. Very familiar and in very general use. Less informal is *Salve*. Italians learning English will often say 'Goodbye' when passing you in the street. This is because they say *Ciao* (or *Addio*) in like circumstances in Italian, while we, of course, say 'Hello'. So remember, *ciao* may be either 'hello' or 'goodbye', according to circumstances. Bear in mind though, that it is familiar style. *Arrivederci* and *Arrivederla* are more suitable for 'goodbye' in most cases, until you are sure just which form to use—and, of course, this is quite simple, as it is really just a matter of repeating back to people what they themselves use to you.

cibo (m). Food (*v.* FOOD).

ciclismo (m). Cycling (*v.* SPORT). One of the national sports of Italy. There is great interest in the famous 'Tours' every year, and in the time and speed track events. The '*Tour de France*' is the *Giro di Francia*, and there is the national *Giro d'Italia*. The leader during the *Giro di Francia* wears the coveted *maglia gialla*, or 'yellow jersey'. The distance cycled in one day of the tour is a *tappa*, that is, a lap in the sense of a part of the total distance. Otherwise one lap, being once round the circuit, is a *giro*. 'To sprint' is *scattare*, and when the winner and those near him arrive, the main body of runners-up, usually all in a lump, are called the *plotone*. A 'track' is *una pista*. 'A cyclist' is *un ciclista*.

ciliegia (f). Cherry (*v.* FOOD).

cilindro (m). Cylinder (*v.* CARS). *Blocco cilindri* (m) is 'cylinder block' and *testa cilindro* (f) is the 'cylinder head'.

cioccolata (f). Chocolate (*v.* FOOD).

cioè. 'That is to say', or 'namely'. For example: *Per molti abitanti della città, e cioè per tutti quelli che abitano vicino alla stazione, il problema è grave*, 'For many inhabitants of the town, that's to say, for all those who live near the station, the problem is a grave one'. *La domenica e gli altri giorni di festa, la città ospita trecentomila persone, cioè ha una popolazione sei volte più numerosa di quella invernale*, 'On Sundays and other holidays the town houses three hundred thousand people, that is, it has six times the population it has during the winter'. *Il cane lappa, cioè prende l'acqua con la lingua*, 'The dog laps, that is, drinks water with the tongue'.

cipolla (f). Onion (*v.* FOOD). 'Garlic' is *aglio*, and 'leek' is *porro*.

clichè (m). Stencil (*v.* OFFICE).

cofano (m). The bonnet of a car.

colpire. 'To hit', 'to punch'.

colpo (m). Blow (such as is struck). *Di colpo* gives the idea of 'suddenly' or 'sharply'. If someone has done something just to make an impression, you say *L'ha fatto per far colpo*.

coltello (m). Knife. *Un coltello a molla* is 'a clasp knife'. 'A hunting knife' is *un coltello da caccia*.

combattimento (m). Fight, contest (*v.* SPORT).

combinare. According to the dictionary, 'to combine' when used transitively, and 'to be agreed on' when used intransitively. Actually, this verb is very often used, and usually with the meaning of 'to arrange', 'to do', sometimes perhaps in rather a bad sense. *Cosa hanno combinato loro due adesso?* 'And what have those two got up to now?'

come. I don't intend to say very much about this adverb, as you will doubtless already be able to manipulate it very well. Note the expression: *Come no*, meaning 'Of course'. *Posso usare la sua matita un attimo?—Sì, come no.* 'May I use your pencil just a moment?'—'Yes, of course'. Then note the exclamation

Com'è bella! 'How beautiful she/it is!' Note also the use of *Come?* instead of *Pardon?* or *Che dice?* And lastly, remember that when you want to say 'as if', *come se*, you must use the subjunctive.   *Comanda la gente come se   fosse il capo,* 'He orders the people about as if he were the boss'.

commedia (f). This can be misleading, as the Italian *commedia* is not only what we call a 'comedy', but a 'play' in general. However, when you know enough Italian to go to an Italian theatre, if possible, you will already certainly know enough to realize this.

commendatore (m). It is useless to give a translation of this word. In many parts of Italy you will frequently hear it used by a person of somewhat lowly station speaking to someone who hasn't really a handle to his name, but for whom the speaker wishes to show his respect. *Buon giorno, commendatore* is something you'll often hear in Italian bars. You will also hear variations, usually *avvocato, direttore* and *dottore*. If Rome had as many lawyers as the people addressed as such in her coffee-bars, they'd outnumber even the priests by about five to one!

commessa (f). Shop assistant (*v.* SHOPS).

compositore (m). The two alternatives are 'composer' and 'compositor'. Somewhat misleading perhaps, although the context would obviously show you which word was the correct one, in almost every case.

comune (m). As a noun, this may mean a 'town' or a 'parish', or it may refer to the administration of these. *Il Comune di Roma* does not refer to the communist enclave in this part of Italy, but is 'The City Administration'. It is also the building where this is housed. Note at the same time that the 'Mayor' of a town is the *Sindaco*, which never seems to sound right to English ears.

comunicazione (f). Message or communication. Notice the single *m* in the Italian spelling.

comunque. One of those extremely common words used in all sorts of circumstances. It means 'however', 'anyway', 'in any case', 'at any rate', 'still'. It is usually an alternative to *in ogni modo. Ha promesso di venire. Comunque non ho troppa fiducia in quello che dice, quindi non aspetterò per molto tempo.* This is 'He has promised to come. However, I don't bank too much on what he says, so I'm not going to wait very long'. *A che ora viene?—Non so ancora. Comunque viene senz'altro.* This would be: 'What time is he coming?'—'I don't know yet, but he's certainly coming, anyway'. One more example: *Ho perso molti soldi oggi. Comunque ce n'ho ancora abbastanza per mangiare'.* 'I've lost a lot of money today. Still, I've got enough left to eat, at any rate'.

condensatore (m). Condenser (*v.* CARS).

condotta (f). This is a 'water pipe'. A *condotto*, on the other hand, is generally something larger, such as 'conduit', 'pipeline', 'sewer'.

conducente (m). Driver (*v.* CARS). A chauffeur is *un autista*.

conferenza (f). Another word to stop yourself from using in the wrong place. A *conferenza* is normally a 'lecture', so if you go to an Italian *conferenza*, don't think that you may be called upon to speak. On the other hand, the English 'conference' can be called a *congresso*.

confezione (f). Again, have a care. If you buy *confezioni* you will not be getting 'confectionery', for which you should say *caramelle* (sweets) or something similar.   *Confezioni* generally refers to ready-made clothes.

coniglio (m). Rabbit (*v.* FOOD).

cono (m). An ice-cream cone, as well as being a 'cone'.   An ice-cream cone can also be a *cornetto*.

conserva (f). Jam (*v.* FOOD). A road traffic jam is *una congestione*. To jam on the brakes is *bloccare i freni*.

contabilità (f). Accounting or accounts department (*v.* OFFICE).

contachilometri (m). Stretching the point a little, this is a 'milometer' or 'mileage indicator' (*v.* CARS).

contatore (m). Meter. *Contatore per elettricità* is 'electricity meter'.

conto (m). The bill. To ask the waiter to bring the bill, you say *Per favore, mi faccia il conto*.   The tip you may leave the waiter, by the way, is called *la mancia*. *Fare una cosa per conto suo* is 'to do something by (or for) oneself'. *L'ho fatto per conto mio*, 'I did it on my own (off my own bat, of my own initiative, for myself)'. *Adesso facciamo i conti* means 'And now let's settle up'.

controllare. This is a verb to beware of. The usual meaning of it is 'to check', not 'to control'. In English we control people, including ourselves at times, and also vehicles and other machines, as well as controlling animals, the ball in such games as cricket and football, and our thoughts. *Tutto sotto controllo*, 'everything under control'. But we do not go upstairs 'to control' whether the children are asleep, or ring the railway station 'to control' train times, for example. The verb *controllare* would, however, be the correct one to use in Italian, as in other languages, in these and similar circumstances. The corresponding noun is *controllo*, which can be 'check' or 'control' in English according to what is said.

convenire. Here there is a multiplicity of meanings. It can mean 'to call to court', 'to bring a case against'; 'to acknowledge'; 'to establish'; 'to meet (together)'; 'to agree (on)'; 'to be necessary'; 'to be better to', and so on. In practice, the last-mentioned meanings are the important ones. *Conviene farlo subito* is 'It would be best to do it at once' or 'It's advisable to do it right away', or stronger, 'It should be done straight away'. *Non mi conviene* can mean 'I don't like it' in the sense of 'It doesn't suit me'. *Conviene comprarlo da lui* means 'It's as well to buy it from him'. In short, when asking, refusing or offering advice, *convenire* is the word to use.

coperchio (m). Cover (*v.* CARS).

coperta (f). Blanket. A woollen blanket is *una coperta di lana*.

copertone (m). Tyre (*v.* CARS). A tyre can also be called *pneumatico* or *gomma*.

copia (f). Copy (*v.* OFFICE).

copialettere (m). Duplicating machine (*v.* OFFICE).

coppa (f). Cup, in the sense of an award. In a motor, the oil sump is known as *la coppa dell'olio*. Naturally, the cup you drink out of is *una tazza*.

coricarsi. To go to bed. More usual, however, is plain *andare a letto*.

corno (m). Horn. The devil has horns, and the sign of the horns, meaning the devil, is the hand with the thumb holding down the two middle fingers, and with the two outside fingers outstretched. So much for the sign. The word also has this signification, and is used, for example, in the expression: *dire corna a qualcuno*, meaning 'to abuse someone'. Also there is: *dire corna di qualcuno*, which is 'to speak very badly of someone'. And referring more specifically to the sign, you can say *fare le corna a . . .*, 'to ward off the devil', 'to ward off the evil eye'. *Non vedo un corno* means 'I can't see a thing'. Note that *corno* can also have the meaning of 'bump', 'lump'.

corrente (f). Current (*v.* CARS).

corse ippiche (f pl). Horse races (*v.* SPORT). A race is *una corsa*, and the race-course is *l'ippodromo* (m). 'Race' in the sense of 'the human race' is *razza*, *la razza umana*. *Da corsa* means 'race-' or 'racing-'; for example, a racehorse is a *cavallo da corsa*. Also, speaking of short journeys, *corsa* means 'trip' or 'run'.

corsia (f). The 'lane' you mark out on the track to separate the runners (*v.* SPORT). The 'lane' you walk along in the country is a *sentiero* (m), while the old-world little town street is a *vicolo* (m).

cosa (f). 'Thing', as you must be very well aware, and used by Italians with a variety of meanings, as in English, although not quite to such an extent. Naturally, all languages make great use of such a basic word as 'thing'. Note that 'something' may be either *qualche cosa* or else *qualcosa*. The important point to make here is the use of the word *cosa* to replace *che?* or to supplement it as in *che cosa?* when asking a question. *Cosa ha detto?* is perfectly normal for 'What did you say?' *Cosa vuole?* 'What does he (*or* do you) want?' and so on. Note, too, that Italians frequently add *una cosa* after the verb *dire*, as in *Ditemi una cosa*, 'Just tell me' and also after the verbs *sapere*—*Sa una cosa?* more or less 'Would you like to know something?' and *sentire*, 'to hear'. For example, *Senta una cosa*, which means 'Just listen to this'. As indicated above, 'thing' is used more in English than is *cosa* in Italian, and this is largely explained by the fact that Italian has the word *roba*, which corresponds roughly to the English 'things' or 'stuff'. For further explanation, *see under* **roba**.

così. 'In this way', 'like this'. *Si fa così* means 'You do it like this', or else 'You go like this'. *Così così* corresponds to the French *comme ci, comme ça*, 'so so'. *Basta così* means 'That's enough', 'It's all right like that' or 'That will do'. As a question it is just as common. *Basta così?*, 'Is that enough?' 'Is it all right like this?' and so on.

No, *non è mica così* gives the idea of 'No, it's not at all like that'. 'And so on', 'and so forth' can best be rendered into Italian by *e così via*. *Non voglio dire così* is 'I don't want to say that', 'That's not what I want to say'. *Non direi così* is 'I wouldn't go so far as to say that'. *E così via*.

coso (m). I don't know what your particular word is for something whose name you have temporarily forgotten or which escapes you for the moment. 'Just now I saw old what's-his-name', 'Hand me the thingummy, will you' and so on. Just as many English speakers overdo this, so do many Italians. *Ho parlato con coso riguardante coso* would not be thought an extraordinary thing to say by some people. At best *coso* is a useful word when you really do forget a name for the moment.

costoletta (f). Chop, cutlet (*v.* FOOD).

cotogna (f). Quince (*v.* FOOD).

cotone (m). Cotton (*v.* HOUSEHOLD). *Cotone idrofilo* is 'cotton wool'.

credenza (f). Cupboard (*v.* HOUSEHOLD). *Una credenza a muro* is 'a built-in cupboard'.

crema (f). The general word for cream, although *panna* is the word that refers to cream of the whipped variety. *Panna montata* is the full expression. *Una cremeria* is one of the words that can mean 'dairy', which is, however, more usually *latteria*.

crescione (m). Water-cress (*v.* FOOD).

cric (m). Car-jack (*v.* CARS). Also referred to as a *martinetto*.

criticare. To criticize. Watch out for the unreliable *critica* (f). This means 'write-up', 'criticism' or 'review' in a paper, while the English 'critic', the person who makes the criticism, the one who writes the reviews, is called a *critico*. 'A film-critic' is *un critico cinematografico*.

croce (f). A cross. The Red Cross is simply *La Croce Rossa*. When tossing up (the verb is *tirare a sorte*) you say *Testa o croce?*

crocevia (f). Crossroads (*v.* CARS). There is also the word *incrocio*, which refers to a crossroads where the two roads intersect at oblique angles. *Un incrocio a T* is a junction where the three roads more or less form a capital T.

crosta (f). Crust (*v.* FOOD). Also the earth's crust.

cruciverba (f). A crossword puzzle. And simple ones, such as those in '*Paese Sera*', are very useful for practising the language; bear this in mind.

cruscotto (m). The dashboard or instrument panel (*v.* CARS).

cucchiaio (m). Spoon (*v.* HOUSEHOLD). A teaspoon is called a *cucchiaino*. Referring to a measure, *un cucchiaio* means, logically, 'a spoonful'. For example, *un cucchiaio da caffè* is 'a teaspoonful', and a *cucchiaio da tavola* is a 'tablespoonful'.

cucina (f). Kitchen. It also refers to the stove or cooker. For instance, *una cucina elettrica* is 'an electric stove or cooker' (*v.* HOUSEHOLD).

cuffia (f). This is the 'casing' or 'shroud' of a machine. On a radio-telegraph set or a tape-recorder, it means the 'headphones'. *Una cuffia radiatore* is 'a radiator grill' (*v.* CARS).

cuscinetto (m). Bearing. *Un cuscinetto a sfere* is 'a ball bearing' (*v.* CARS).

D

dado (m). Nut (*v.* CARS). The 'bolt' which goes with the nut is called the *bullone* (m).

dai, dagli. Much like *su*, *dai* seeks to encourage. 'Come on, cheer up' is one meaning. At a boxing match you'd expect a shouted *dagli* to mean 'let him have it', and you'd be right. On the whole, *dai* is stronger than *su*, a bit rougher, if you like to look at it this way.

dattero (m). Date, of the sort you eat (*v.* FOOD). 'The date', meaning the day of the year, is, of course, *la data*.

dattilografa (f). Typist (*v.* OFFICE). The verb 'to type' can be *dattilografare*, although in speaking it is much more common to say *scrivere a macchina* or (and this is the most usual) *battere a macchina*.

debole (m). 'Weakness' in the sense of 'weak *or* soft spot'. *La signora Rossi aveva un debole per le persone distinte* means 'Mrs Rossi had a weakness for distinguished people'. You could also say 'have a partiality for' or 'be partial to'. *Lei ha un debole per lui* means 'She has a soft spot for him' or 'She is rather keen on him'. As you will know, *debole* is an ordinary adjective meaning 'weak', 'feeble' and so on. There is an alternative noun, *debolezza* (f): *per quella sua debolezza delle cose francesi*, 'through that weakness of hers for things French'.

decarburare. To decarbonize or decarburize (*v.* CARS).

decidersi. 'To decide, make up one's mind'. *Lei si è decisa già?* is 'Has she made her mind up yet?' *Deciditi!* means 'Make up your mind!' This is all quite straightforward, and put in to remind you that quite often an English expression, commonly used, has a simple English equivalent, which itself is near to the Latin and therefore usually near to the Italian word. So here, instead of translating 'make up your mind', think of 'decide', and there you are.

delitto (m). Crime. *Il luogo del delitto* is 'the scene of the crime'.

delusione (f). Disappointment. You will also find the word *disappunto*, but Italians have more *delusioni* than *disappunti*. The corresponding adjective, also a bit of a false friend, is *deluso*. *Era rimasto deluso di . . .* means 'He was disappointed by . . .'. Note that a 'delusion' is an *illusione* (f).

dentista (m). Dentist (*v.* SHOPS). *Dentiera* (f) is a 'dental plate'.

dettare. To dictate (*v.* OFFICE). 'A dictaphone' is *un dittafono*.

di. With attached article, this of course becomes *del, dei* and so on. This is not going to be a treatise on the many and various ways of using the word *di*. I wish to point out the partitive use—corresponding to English 'some', 'any'. *Mi dia del burro* is 'Give me some butter'. *Ha delle olive?* asks 'Have you any olives?' 'But', someone will say, 'I've heard sentences in Italian where the word is omitted'. Quite so—and all the official grammar book will tell you is that *in italiano si omettono molto spesso in senso partitivo le forme del plurale*. You can therefore say either *Mi dia soldi* or *Mi dia dei soldi*. However, as a general rule, when in doubt, put it in. In practice, there is often a substitute for both singular and plural. Instead of *Mi dia del burro* you often hear *Mi dia un po' di burro*, for example. And, whereas you could say *Ho visto dei soldati*, you would in fact probably say *Ho visto molti soldati* or *un mucchio di soldati*.

differenziale (m). Differential (*v.* CARS). In mathematics, *calcolo differenziale* is 'differential calculus'.

dilettante (m). The word for 'amateur', as opposed to a professional, who is *un professionista*.

dinamo (m). Dynamo (*v.* CARS).

diplomato (m). The adjective *diplomatico* means just what you would expect it to mean. The false friend lurks in the noun *diplomato*, however, as he is someone with a diploma. A *diplomatico* is a 'diplomat'. Note that *un diploma di laurea* (*see* **laurea**) is the equivalent of our degree.

di ricambio. This means 'spare' or 'reserve', as also does *di riserva*. *Un pezzo di ricambio* is 'a spare part', and *una ruota di ricambio* is 'a spare wheel'.

disastro (m). This is a disaster, right enough. It's also a common way of referring to a flop, something that didn't come off well. *È un disastro!* is 'It's terrible!' Note also in this context that *tremendo* (*q.v.*) refers to something bad, if not specifically stating that something is tremendous in size.

disco (m). A gramophone record. *Disco della frizione* is 'clutch disc' (*v.* CARS). *Un disco volante*, if you believe in such things, is 'a flying saucer'.

discorso (m). Speech. *Cambiare discorso* means 'to change the subject'. *Ti dispiace cambiare discorso?* is 'Let's change the subject, if you don't mind'.

discreto. This is one of the grades of, say, knowledge of some subject. Your knowledge may be *ottimo* (excellent), *buono* (good), *discreto* (quite good, satisfactory, moderate), or *mediocre* (sub-standard, unsatisfactory, poor, lacking). Using this adjective in a modest way gives the idea of 'Well, I can't exactly claim to be an expert, but I must say that I'm moderately good' meaning that you do, in fact, have a pretty good opinion of yourself. The adjective 'discreet' is also *discreto*.

discussione (f). A discussion, not usually so quiet and orderly as one in English, perhaps. *Discutere* is the verb.

disgrazia (f). Usually an 'accident' or a 'mishap'. Unfortunately, *una disgrazia non viene mai sola*, 'troubles never come singly'. The noun referring to a person, *un disgraziato*, is frequently heard and corresponds to the English 'wretch', in the sense of some poor, unfortunate person, as well as in the sense of some 'miserable wretch'. So, too, with the adjective, also *disgraziato*. Notice that the English disgrace is more often than not *una vergogna*, literally 'a shame'.

dispiace. The opposite of *piace*. *Mi dispiace* therefore means 'I don't like it'. A very useful expression to use when asking someone whether he minds: *Vi dispiace se apro la finestra?* 'Do you mind if I open the window?' Then again, it is used to mean 'Excuse me' or 'I'm sorry'. Having inconvenienced someone, you say *Mi dispiace*, perhaps after having said *Mi scusi tanto*, and so on. You would say it, for example, on taking leave after having asked someone to do something for you which has taken a bit of time and trouble. 'I'm sorry for the trouble', as it were.

distributore (m). Distributor (*v.* CARS).

ditale (m). Thimble (*v.* HOUSEHOLD).

diva (f). *Diva* is really a 'goddess', but is used in referring to a 'star' of stage or screen.

diventare. To become, to get, to grow. *È diventata molto magra* means 'She has got very thin'. Note, however, that the verb *rimanere* (*q.v.*) is often used in the sense of 'to get', as in the sentence *Sono rimasto molto male*, 'I was (got) very disappointed'. *Diventare pazzo di . . .* is 'to get mad (*or* crazy) about . . .'.

diverso. Just to remind you that this adjective can mean 'different' just as much as it means 'various' or 'several'. English speakers tend to use the word *differente* a little too often, overlooking that *diverso* is not infrequently the best word to use. *Sembra molto diverso adesso* is 'It seems very different now'.

divertirsi. 'To enjoy or amuse oneself'. *Mi sono divertito molto ieri al ballo* is 'I enjoyed myself very much at the dance yesterday'. The corresponding noun is *divertimento*. To a friend going off to the cinema, for example, you would say: *Buon divertimento*—'Have a good time', 'Enjoy yourself'.

doccia (f). Shower, shower-bath (*v.* HOUSEHOLD).

dolce. Sweet, both as an adjective and as a noun (m).

dolci (m pl). Dessert, sweet (*v.* FOOD).

dorso (m). Back. With reference to swimming, this is the 'back stroke' (*v.* SPORT).

drogheria (f). Don't try to call this a 'druggery' or anything fancy like this. Different books will give you different things for a *drogheria*, and it is really quite difficult to pin it down precisely, but the nearest translation would be 'a general store'. If you say 'grocer's', you have a case, as you can buy certain eatables in certain *drogherie*, but it is generally stretching the point a bit. In a *drogheria* you can buy the following: cotton wool, toothpaste, shampoo, disinfectant, soap powder, toilet soap, brooms, brushes, herbs, coffee beans, perfume, dried fruit—so perhaps you can make up your own mind what translation you would like to give the word.

due passi (m). *Fare due passi* is 'to have a bit of a stroll'.

due punti (m). Colon (*v.* OFFICE). 'A semi-colon' is *punto e virgola*.

dunque. This usually corresponds to 'well', although most dictionaries will tell you that it is 'then', 'so', 'consequently' and so on. If you ask someone how long another person has been there, for instance, the answer might well be *È stato qui* *dunque cinque ore*, 'He's been here, well (let me see) five hours'. Some people begin a good many of their sentences with this word. *Dunque, me ne vado fra poco*; *Dunque, cosa pensate fare adesso?* and so on.

E

ebbene. 'Well then', 'all the same'. Look at these examples: *Qui il mare è meno indicato per esibirsi come tuffatore. Ebbene, non passa settimana che qualcuno non si faccia male con un tuffo.* This could be translated: 'Here the sea is less suitable for showing off one's diving abilities. All the same, not a week goes by without someone's hurting himself diving.' Again: *Ho detto che non devi comprare tante caramelle. Ebbene, se tu vuoi rovinare i tuoi denti . . .* (I've told you not to buy so many sweets. All right then, if you want to ruin your teeth . . . ').

ecco. Every learner of Italian should be aware of the first meaning of *ecco*, 'here . . . is', in the same way that *voici* and *voilà* are used in French. *Eccolo* in the usual way means 'Here he is' or 'Here it is'. If someone or something is espied in the distance, then *Eccolo* is 'There he is' or 'There it is'. Giving someone something, *Ecco* becomes 'Here you are'. In a conversation, the word is very frequently used. *Non mi ricordo come si chiama quella ragazza.—Si chiama Eleonora o qualche cosa così, non è vero?—Sì, ecco, adesso mi ricordo che si chiama Leonora.* ('I can't remember that girl's name'. 'It's Eleonora or something like that, isn't it?' 'Yes, that's it, now I remember, it's Leonora.') Again, *È un animale che somiglia molto a un cavallo, con strisce; anzi, assomiglia a una zebra, ecco.* 'It's an animal that very closely resembles a horse, with stripes; or rather it resembles a zebra, to be more precise.' Another example: *Siete un bugiardo, ecco quello che siete!* 'You're a liar, that's what you are!'

You will notice that *ecco* is often put at the end of a sentence, to confirm something (something like 'mark you', or the Welsh 'look you'), or even as an afterthought. *Non si può dire che non è giusto, ma, insomma, come direi? . . . non è sempre corretto, ecco.* ('You can't say it's not right, but all the same, what should I say? . . . well, it's not always correct, you see.')

Just one or two further examples: *Come, non basta così? Bene, gliene do ancora due, ecco. Va bene così?* 'What, isn't this enough? All right, I'll give you two more, look. Is that all right now?' *Avete una camicia grigia?—Ecco una camicia di colore più o meno grigio* ('Have you a grey shirt?' 'Here's a shirt of a more or less grey colour'). And finally a few expressions using *ecco*:

Ecco tutto, That's all
Ecco fatto, That's that

Eccolo che arriva, Here he comes
Ecco di che si tratta, That's what it's about
Eccone abbastanza, That's enough of that

edicola (f). Bookstall, kiosk, newspaper stand (*v.* SHOPS).

educato. This adjective does not always necessarily refer to one's
school education. In fact, it more likely points to one's
manners, meaning 'polite, well-mannered'. 'Education' in the
school sense is more *istruzione*, and therefore 'educated' can
be *istruito*. According to the context, however, it may possibly
be *educato*.

elenco (m). The normal word for 'list', which can also be *lista*.
L'elenco telefonico is 'the telephone directory' (*v.* OFFICE).

elettricità (f). Electricity (*v.* HOUSEHOLD). Note that a 'switch' is
interruttore, and 'to turn' is *girare*, but *girare l'interruttore*
merely indicates the mechanical action of turning, while the
whole action of 'turning off the light' and 'turning on the
light' are indicated by the verbs *spegnere la luce* and *accendere
la luce*.

emozione (f). 'Emotion', if you like, but more likely to be
'excitement'. The idea we get from such a sentence as 'His
face betrayed his emotion' is best rendered by *Era visibilmente
commosso*.

entrare. To enter. Remember that Italian has the construction
'to enter into a room', that is, *entrare in una stanza*. *Non
c'entra* means 'He (*or* she *or* it) doesn't enter into it'. The
corresponding noun is *entrata* (f), which may refer to an
entrance in the sense of a door or to one in the sense of the
going in, or else the entrance which refers to the money you
pay to go in. In book-keeping, *entrate e uscite* are 'credit and
debit'.

eppure. 'Yet', 'still', 'nevertheless'. *Disse che non veniva, eppure
è arrivato proprio adesso* means 'He said he wouldn't come,
and yet he's just arrived'.

erbivendolo (m). Greengrocer (*v.* SHOPS). Also *fruttivendolo* and
fruttaiolo.

esercizio (m). Exercise or practice. *Mantenersi in esercizio* means
'to keep in practice'. Notice that *l'esercito* (m) is 'the Army'.
Fare il servizio militare is 'to do military service'.

eventualmente. Another false friend, not meaning 'eventually'
(which can be *finalmente* or *alla fine*), but 'perhaps', 'possibly'.
Viene stasera? 'Are you coming this evening?' may receive
the answer: *Eventualmente*, 'Perhaps', meaning that whether
or not the person comes is conditional on something else.

F

fabbrica (f). A factory, for which do not say *fattoria*, which is 'a farm'. 'A fabric' is *un tessuto*.

fabbricare. Just as *una fabbrica* is 'a factory', so *fabbricare* is 'to produce' (in a factory), 'to manufacture'. Dictionaries go on repeating the old mistake of saying that the verb means 'to fabricate'. If we are agreed that 'to fabricate' means 'to invent a story', *i.e.* 'to lie', then this is, in Italian, *falsificare* or *dire bugie* or *inventare*.

faccenda (f). *Una faccenda* is 'a matter', 'a bit of business' etc. It can be translated 'thing' or even 'story' according to the expression as, for example, *No, questa è un'altra faccenda*, 'No, that's quite a different story'. *Faccende domestiche* are 'household duties' or 'chores'. *Non capisco niente di questa faccenda* is 'I don't understand a thing about this business'. *Una brutta faccenda* is 'a bad business'.

faccia (f). Face. *Faccia tosta* is 'effrontery', 'brazenness'.

fagiano (m). Pheasant (*v.* FOOD).

fagiolo (m). This is a bean of the haricot variety (*v.* FOOD). 'Beans' may otherwise be *fave* (f pl).

falegname (m). Carpenter (*v.* SHOPS). Also a 'joiner'. 'Carpentry' and 'joinery' work may both be *falegnameria*, although the word *carpenteria* also exists.

fallimento (m). Bankruptcy or failure. Noted here for its idiomatic use in, for instance *Sono stato alla riunione, ma è stato un fallimento*, 'I went to the meeting, but it was a complete failure'.

fanale (m). Light. In the sense of *faro* (m), *fanale* means 'head-light'. An aircraft navigation light is *un fanale d'ala*. 'A tail light' on a vehicle is called *un fanale di coda*. *Fanali laterali* are 'side lights'. *Un fanalino* is, as its name suggests, 'a little light', and *un fanalino rosso posteriore* is 'a red rear lamp'. The light on or by the number plate is called *fanaletto di targa*.

fare. *Fare* more often means 'to make' than 'to do', although it can mean either. And apart from these two basic meanings, there are several expressions, which deserve to be stressed, where *fare* corresponds to another verb in English.

    fare attenzione, to be careful
    fare caldo (freddo), to be warm (cold) (of weather)
    fare colazione, to have breakfast
    fare male, to hurt
    fare una passeggiata, to go for a walk
    fare una visita, to pay a visit
    (non) fare a meno di, not to help

fare fuori, to kill, 'bump off'
fare il conto, to get the bill ready
far fare qualche cosa, to have something done

Here are a few examples of sentences:
Non avevo ancora fatto colazione, 'I hadn't yet had breakfast'.
Non potei fare a meno di sentire tutta la conversazione, 'I couldn't help hearing the whole conversation'.
Cameriere, faccia il conto, 'Waiter, please bring the bill'.

If you wish to be informed of something, you may leave instructions for someone to 'let me know when he arrives', for example. This would be *Fammi sapere quando arriverà, per piacere*. If you are not bothered one way or the other about something, you may well say *Fa lo stesso*. If something makes you sick, nauseates you, you would be using a very common, if somewhat slangy, expression if you said *Mi fa schifo*. And lastly—although it would be possible to go on and on with this verb, in the same way that you could go on and on with the English verb 'to get', notice the construction *fare meglio a (non) fare una cosa*, 'to have better (not) do something'. For instance: *Farebbe molto meglio a non toccarlo*, 'You had far better not touch it'.

Fare la maglia, fare la calza, mean 'to knit', 'to do some knitting' (*v.* HOUSEHOLD). *Far girare con la manovella di avviamento* is 'to crank' (by hand) (*v.* CARS).

farfalla (f). In swimming, this is 'the butterfly stroke' (*v.* SPORT). To a motorcyclist, however, *la farfalla* is 'the throttle', and *aprire la farfalla* is 'to open the throttle'. On the other hand, *una farfalla* is an ordinary 'butterfly', unless you make her into *una farfalla di baco da seta*, in which case she is 'a silk-worm'.

farina (f). Flour (*v.* FOOD).

farmacia (f). Pharmacy or chemist's (*v.* SHOPS). *Un dottore in farmacia* is 'a pharmacist'.

faro (m). On a car, this is a 'headlight' (*v.* CARS). On an aerodrome, a *faro* would be a 'beacon', while at sea it is a 'lighthouse'.

fastidio (m). 'Bother', something that puts you out or upsets you. The adjective is *fastidioso*, meaning 'irksome', 'upsetting', 'off-putting' or 'tiresome', perhaps also 'fussy'. *Mi dà troppo fastidio* means 'It annoys me too much'. *Le dà fastidio?* asks 'Does this bother you?' The verb *infastidire* means 'to molest', 'to annoy'.

fattoria (f). This is the usual word for 'a farm'. Don't confuse it with 'a factory', which is *una fabbrica* (*q.v.*).

fattorino (m). Nothing to do with little farm boys or anything like that. This means 'messenger', boy or man; an errand-boy is also *fattorino*.

fattura (f). Invoice (*v.* OFFICE). There is also a verb, *fatturare*, 'to invoice'.

favore (m). You may use this to mean 'favour', instead of using *piacere*; but the point I want to stress here is that you should not overdo the *per favore* business. I've heard Englishmen in shops asking for several articles, saying *per favore* after each item (and often before it, too!). This sounds strange in Italian. Be polite, of course, but check yourself from doing *per favore* to death.

fegato (m). Liver (*v.* FOOD). Accent on first syllable.

femmina (f). Female. It can mean 'a woman', although it sounds somewhat pejorative. The best translation of the title of the film called '*Femmine di Lusso*' would, I suppose, be 'Females de Luxe'. A male, on the other hand, is *un maschio*. Asking whether it is a boy or a girl, you should say *femmina o maschio?*

fermaglio (m). Paper clip (*v.* OFFICE).

fermare. To stop. Reflexively, *fermarsi* (*v.* CARS). Basically, *fermare* means 'to stop' or else 'to fasten'. In giving instructions to a taxi-driver, you'd have to use this verb to tell him to stop: *Si fermi qui* (and to tell him to turn, rather than say *tornare*, say *girare*. *Tornare indietro* is 'to turn back'). A bus will stop at a *fermata* (which may or may not be *a richiesta*). We are reminded of the French *Ferme çà* by *Fermi là*, 'Stop there'. *Fermarsi per una settimana in un albergo* is 'to put up at a hotel for a week'. *Senza mai fermarsi* is 'without ever stopping'.

Ferragosto (m). This is the August bank holiday. The fifteenth of August, the feast of the Assumption, is the specific day of the holiday, although it is quite common for the whole week to be taken as a holiday. It is usual for all shops to close on the fifteenth, and in fact many shops close for the summer holidays for a week or two during this period. This is a general holiday throughout Italy and visitors to Rome will find it almost dead, while those who visit the seaside resorts will have to fight to find a place. Road users are constantly urged, on the radio and on television, to be extremely prudent over the Ferragosto period—but road deaths are still pretty high on the fifteenth and the days thereabouts.

ferro (m). Iron, both the metal and the household implement. 'An electric iron' is *un ferro da stiro elettrico*. The verb 'to iron' is *stirare*.

fetta (f). Slice (*v.* FOOD). In the case of bacon, 'rasher'. The diminutive is *fettina*, also meaning 'slice'.

fiacca (f). This summons up the idea of 'tired, listless blood', warm, damp winds, general limpness and laziness. Actually, it's a word which the Italians have presented to Argentine Spanish, in which language it is now used much more than in Italian itself. *Essere fiacco* corresponds to the French *J'ai la flemme*, 'I feel lazy', 'I can't be fagged' etc.

fiammifero (m). The sort of 'match' that you strike. Note, however, that the sort of matches most used in Italy are tiny ones called *cerini*, minute waxed sticks which take some people some time to get used to. A close second in popularity are book-matches, usually referred to by their registered trade name—*fiammiferi Minerva*. Note, too, that the 'match' played between two teams is *una partita*.

ficcare. *Ficcarsi* is 'to hide oneself somewhere'. The basic idea of *ficcare* is 'to stick *or* thrust something somewhere'. You can stick your nose into someone else's business (*ficcare il naso negli affari altrui*), stick your hands into your pockets (*ficcare le mani in tasca*) and so forth.

fico (m). Fig (*v.* FOOD). *See also* under **importare**.

figura (f). Just to remind you that this does not primarily refer to the 'figure', but to the 'appearance' in general. And note the very popular expressions, *fare una bella figura* and *fare una brutta figura* which mean respectively 'to cut a good figure' ('to keep up appearances', more or less, but rather stronger), and 'to let yourself down, to make a bad impression'. In Italy, it is important to present a façade, to have people think that you are making the magnificent gesture, doing the right thing and so on. You should not *fare una brutta figura*, ' make a bad impression'. If you are the director of a firm, don't think that you may cycle to work, as this would be making a very *brutta figura*. I should say that fear of a *brutta figura* is stronger than the desire to make a *bella figura*. In many countries, the sight of the director on a bicycle would cause people to comment 'A bit eccentric', 'Doing it for his health', 'Had his licence endorsed, I suppose' and so forth. But to Italians it is definitely 'a bad show'. *La linea* is more the figure women watch and men whistle at—if it's not called plainly *corpo*.

figurarsi. 'To imagine', 'to think', 'to fancy'. Most frequently used as a sort of exclamation. *Figuratevi che . . . !* 'Just imagine . . . !' Look at these sentences: *Pensavi farlo veramente?* ('Did you really mean to do it?')—*Ma no, figurati!* ('No, of course I didn't!'). *Che cosa voleva?—Figurati cosa poteva volere!* ('What did he want?'—'You can just imagine what he wanted!')

filetto (m). This may be either the 'thread' of a screw, or else a 'fillet' (*v.* FOOD).

filo (m). 'Wire', the sort made of metal. It may also be the 'filament'. Another possibility is 'yarn' or 'thread' in a textile context. *Filo spinato* is 'barbed wire'. *Filo di rame isolato* is 'insulated copper wire' (*v.* CARS).

filobus (m). Trolley-bus.

filtro (m). Filter. A *filtro aria* is an 'air cleaner' or 'filter' (*v.* CARS).

finestrino (m). This is obviously the diminutive of 'window'. It means 'little window', and is especially used for cars. *Un finestrino con vetro abbassabile* is 'a drop window'. *Finestrino posteriore* is 'rear window'.

fondo (m). 'Base', 'bottom', 'lower part' of something. The *fondo cassa* is the office 'float', the 'cash in hand'. *In fondo* is a common expression, giving the idea of 'when all's said and done', 'at heart', or 'fundamentally'. *Ma, in fondo, è una brava ragazza* means 'But she's really a good girl, basically'.

foglio (m). Sheet (of paper, and of metal, for example). Note that the sheet you put on the bed is *un lenzuolo*. And be careful to distinguish between a *foglio* (m) and *una foglia* (f), which is the sort of leaf you find on trees.

folle. Neutral (position of gears). *In folle* is 'in neutral'.

forare. 'To drill' or 'to puncture'. *Una foratura* may be 'drilling' or 'a puncture' (*v.* CARS).

forbici (f pl). Scissors. *Forbici per le unghie* are 'nail scissors'. *Forbici da giardino* are 'garden shears'.

forcella (f). Fork, of the sort you have on a motorbike. Remember that the fork with which you eat your food is *una forchetta*, while the fork where one road divides to become two is *un bivio*.

formaggio (m). Cheese. French speakers, beware of the order of the first few letters. Just as in English we may ask for 'half a pound of Dutch', so in Italian certain sorts of cheese need not be specifically referred to as *formaggio*. You refer to Parmesan cheese, for example, as *parmigiano*, while you say just *groviera* for 'Gruyère', at the same time specifying whether you want imported *svizzera* or Italian-made *nazionale*.

formazione (f). Formation. In football, this would be the 'line-up' (*v.* SPORT).

forno (m). This may be 'oven', 'stove', 'kiln' or 'furnace', according to circumstances. The diminutive, *fornello*, means 'hot-plate'. *Fornello elettrico* is 'electric hot-plate' and *fornello a gas* is 'gas hot-plate' (*v.* HOUSEHOLD).

forza (f). Strength or force. The point of including this word is to indicate how much it is used in everyday speech to encourage people. At a football match, for example, you may hear the shout, *Forza, Roma!* meaning 'Come on, Rome!' 'Play up, Rome!' And it isn't a word to be merely shouted. You often hear the spoken encouragement being given to people. Notice in this context the use of *su* and *dai* (*q.v.*). Another point worth mentioning is the use of the expression *per forza*. *Per forza* can mean 'by force', *i.e.* 'not willingly', or else 'necessarily'. This second alternative is very common. *Devo venire questa sera per forza* is 'I *have* to come this evening'.

Lui deve pagare domani, non è vero? means 'He should pay tomorrow, shouldn't he?' and the answer might be *Sì, per forza, perchè se no, non possiamo partire,* 'Yes, he *must*, otherwise we can't leave'.

fragola (f). Strawberry (*v.* FOOD).

fra parentesi. In brackets, in parentheses. 'To put in brackets' is *mettere fra parentesi* (*v.* OFFICE).

fregare. The first meaning of this verb is 'to rub'. However, this is one of those words adopted by the lower strata of society and given the double and contradictory treatment of mystification and diversity of clear meaning. You can pin it down to several clear-cut meanings, yet the adept users of this word will still smile a wicked smile and keep something back from you. *Fregare* can be used in the expression *Me ne frego,* corresponding to the French *'Je m'en fiche',* 'I don't give a damn'. Then, in slang, *fregare* can be 'to pinch, to steal, to knock off'. 'To cheat' is another possibility.

frenare. To brake, to put the brakes on (*v.* CARS). When you brake hard, you make *una frenata,* 'a putting on of the brakes'. A *freno* is a 'brake', of which *freno a mano* is a 'hand-brake' and *freno a pedale* is a 'foot-brake'.

friggere. To fry (*v.* FOOD). The past participle is *fritto,* so that *un uovo fritto* is 'a fried egg'.

frigorifero (m). Refrigerator (*v.* HOUSEHOLD).

frizione (f). Clutch (*v.* CARS). *Innestare la frizione* means 'to engage the clutch', while the opposite, 'to disengage the clutch', is *disinnestare* (or *distaccare*) *la frizione.* 'Friction drive' is *trasmissione a frizione.*

fruttivendolo (m). Greengrocer (*v.* SHOPS).

fungo (m). Mushroom (*v.* FOOD). You find 'mushrooms' of the cut-up variety much used in Italy, forming part of many dishes. Notice particularly that they are often put on the top of a *pizza—pizza con funghi.*

furbo. This adjective indicates that someone is 'smart', 'crafty', 'clever', 'cunning', 'artful'. *Non fare il furbo* is 'Don't try to be clever'.

fusto (m). Not a very useful word, this, you'll probably say to yourself. The dictionary says that it means 'barrel, cask'. The colloquial application is otherwise, however. A *fusto* is the sort who likes to show off his muscles to everybody. He'll make a point of wearing a short-sleeved shirt, and an open collar to show the hair on his chest, and he'll stand on a bus even if there's plenty of room to sit, because he wants to hang on the rail and show his biceps and so on. There was a film called *Il Grande Fusto,* 'The Great Show-Off'.

G

gabinetto (m). This means a 'closet' in general, applied especially to the *gabinetto di toeletta*, the 'w.c.' (*v.* HOUSEHOLD).

gamba (f). Leg. In Italian you are not able to 'pull the leg', that is, to use the word 'leg' in the expression that conveys this idea, which is, in fact, *prendere in giro*, 'to take in a circle'. Notice the very much-used expression, *in gamba*. It's quite a compliment to be referred to as being *in gamba*, as this means that you know what you're doing, that you know how to put things across, that you are good at your job, that you are 'one of the boys' and so on. *È un tipo molto in gamba* means, to stretch the translation a bit, 'He's no square', 'He knows his onions'.

gamberetto (m). Shrimp (*v.* FOOD).

gambero (m). Prawn (*v.* FOOD). *Scampi* are, of course, the sea-food (*frutti di mare*) of this type most referred to.

ganascia (f) **del freno.** Brake shoe (*v.* CARS).

gancio (m). Hook, both one made of metal and the one in the boxer's armoury (*v.* SPORT).

gara (f). Match, event, contest, competition (*v.* SPORT). *Una gara femminile* is 'a ladies' event', while 'men's event' is *gara maschile*.

gelateria (f). Ice-cream shop. Often an ordinary 'bar'. Here you buy a *gelato*, an 'ice-cream', or perhaps a *granita*, the sort of ice with a fruit flavour and without cream.

gelatina (f). Jelly (*v.* FOOD).

geniale. Here is another one of the words which can easily be confused. In Italian the adjective means 'of genius', while the English 'genial' is *cordiale* in Italian.

getto (m). Jet (*v.* CARS).

gettone (m). Counter, chip, or token. If you wish to make a phone-call, or travel on the Rome underground (*la Metropolitana*), you buy a *gettone* (at a bar, or at a newspaper kiosk, respectively), and use the slotted token in the apparatus. The telephone *gettone* will cost you 30 lire, for instance.

ghiaccio (m). Ice. The ice or 'rime' that collects on the wings of aircraft is also *ghiaccio*. 'Iced water' is *acqua ghiacciata*.

già. As you must know, this means 'already'. *Il treno è già arrivato* means 'The train has already arrived'. But you will hear this word a lot more than you might think, as it is very often used to mean 'Yes, that's right'. *Quella ragazza è una civetta irrecuperabile.—Già!* ('That girl's a terrible flirt'. 'Yes, she is' *or* 'You've said a mouthful'). In this way it is often used double—*Già, già*, to enhance the effect.

giallo (m & adj). As an adjective this means 'yellow', of course. As a noun, however, apart from perhaps meaning 'egg-yolk', this word refers to a detective film or detective story. *Ho visto un giallo stupendo ieri sera* means 'I saw a wonderful detective film last night'.

giallorossi (m pl). Literally, the 'yellow-reds'. These are the colours of Rome Football Club, and members of the team are referred to as *i giallorossi* (collectively) and *un giallorosso* (individually). Milan F.C. are *i rossoneri*—and note that this is the usual way of referring nickname fashion to Italian football teams.

giavellotto (m). Javelin. The sport is known as *lancio del giavellotto*.

ginnasio (m). Watch this false friend. The word means 'secondary school', 'grammar school', 'high school'. The place where you do gymnastic exercises, the English 'gymnasium', is *una palestra*.

giocare. To play (*v.* SPORT). 'A player' is *un giocatore*. The thing a child plays with, the plaything or toy, is *un giocattolo*.
'A game' is *un gioco*.

gioielleria (f). Jeweller's (*v.* SHOPS).

girare. To turn, used transitively. *Girare un angolo* is 'to turn a corner'. Intransitively, it means 'to turn (itself) round'. *Mi gira la testa* means 'My head's in a whirl'; *ha girato abbastanza* gives the idea that 'He's knocked around quite a bit'. The corresponding noun is *giro*, 'a turn'. *Andare in giro* is 'to go round'. *Essere in giro* means 'to be around'. *Il capo è in giro* means 'The boss is about'. A *giro* often refers to a trip or tour. *Vado a fare un giro per la città* is 'I'm going to have a walk round the town'. *Mio cugino sta facendo un giro in Francia* means 'My cousin is making a tour in France'. On top of all this we have the well-worn phrase *prendere qualcuno in giro*, 'to pull the leg, to take the Mickey'. *Ci sta prendendo in giro* is 'You are pulling our legs'.
The famous '*Tour de France*' is called, in Italian, *Il giro di Francia*, while the Italian 'tour' is *Il giro d'Italia*.

gita (f). 'Trip' or 'excursion'. *Una gita turistica* is 'a tourist excursion'.

giunto (m). Joint. The universal joint is *giunto universale* (*v.* CARS).

giusto. This adjective means 'just', 'fair', 'suitable', 'fit' and 'proper'. You often hear people using it to say 'That's right'. *Sì, è giusto*, 'Yes, it's quite right'. It may also be an adverb, in the following way: *giusto in questo momento*, 'just at this moment'.

gol (m). Goal (*v.* SPORT).

gomma (f). Tyre (*v.* CARS) or rubber (*v.* OFFICE). Other words for 'tyre' are: *pneumatico* and *copertone* (m). *Una gomma da inchiostro* is 'an ink-rubber'.

granchio (m). Crab (*v.* FOOD).

granchiolino (m). Crayfish (*v.* FOOD).

grasso (m). Animal, vegetable or chemical fat. Also 'grease' (*v.* CARS).

grazie. As pointed out in the case of *per favore*, you can easily overdo using this. English speakers tend to thank a great deal, and the word *grazie* is sometimes out of place in Italian. An unexpected *grazie*, in a shop for example, often receives the comment *grazie (a) lei* stressing the *lei*. However, if you do use it too much, or rather, more than is natural, you are erring on the right side, of course. *Grazie tanto* is a common combination, meaning 'Thank you very much'.

groviera (f). *See* **formaggio.**

guaio (m). A 'mess', a 'spot of trouble', an 'embarrassing situation', a 'difficulty'. *Un bel guaio* is 'a nice mess'. *Passare un brutto guaio* is 'to have a spot of serious trouble'. *La ragazza è nei guai* means 'The girl is in trouble'. *Ho perso il mio porta-foglio: è un guaio* means 'I've lost my brief-case, so I'm in trouble'. *Ostia ha i suoi guai, ma offre ai Romani la comodità di avere il mare a due passi* ('Ostia has some drawbacks, but it offers Romans the convenience of having the seaside on their doorstep.').

guanciale (m). Pillow (*v.* HOUSEHOLD).

guasto (m). Breakdown, failure (*v.* CARS). Lifts and slot machines which are out of order will have the word *guasto* written on a card and placed on them.

guida (f). 'Guide', in the sense of one who accompanies visitors round the town and so on. Also in the general sense, something to be guided by. *Una scuola di guida* is 'a driving school'. Note that the verb *guidare* means 'to drive'. *Non sa guidare* is 'He can't drive'. *Rosanna sta prendendo lezioni di guida* means 'Rosanna is taking driving lessons'. Another thing to note is that *la guida telefonica* is 'the telephone directory', otherwise called the *elenco telefonico*.

I

idea (f). Idea. *Cambiare idea* means 'to change your mind'. *Avere idea di* is 'to have some idea of'. *Ottima idea* is 'excellent idea'.

idraulico (m). The hydraulics man, or, to be less posh, the plumber. This is the word usually written outside the shop, while the plumber is normally referred to as the *stagnaio* (m).

ignorare. A misleading word, meaning 'not to know', 'not to realize'. *Lei non ignorava che egli aveva lasciato Milano in compagnia di Luigi* means 'She was not unaware that he had left Milan together with Luigi'. 'To ignore someone' is usually *far finta d'ignorare* or *non fare attenzione* a . . . .

imbroglio (m). This can be a 'mix-up', 'tangle' or 'scrape', or 'difficulty', but summons up in the minds of most Italians the idea of 'trick' or 'fraud'. The verb is *imbrogliare*, generally meaning 'to swindle', 'to cheat', 'to defraud'.

imbucare. Don't go getting involved with *andare alla posta con questa lettera* or things like this. Just put the letter in the hole, as they say in Italian. *Vado a imbucare queste lettere* means 'I'm going to post these letters'.

imminente. This means 'imminent', but you will often see it on film advertisement posters, to tell you that the film is 'coming shortly'.

immondizia (f). 'Rubbish', 'refuse' or 'garbage'. 'Garbage' more in the sense of 'what is swept up', rather than 'filth, muck', is *spazzatura* (f). The 'dustman' is the *spazzino*. *Gettò il sasso su un mucchio d'immondizia* would be 'He threw the stone on to a heap of rubbish'.

impiegato (m). 'Clerk' or 'employee', from the verb *impiegare*, 'to employ', 'to use, make use of'.

importare. *Non importa* means 'It doesn't matter'. *Mi importa un fico secco* means 'I don't care two hoots'. For this last expression we also have *Me ne infischio*, while across the borderline into slang we have *Me ne frego*, from the verb *fregare* (*q.v.*).

inchiostro (m). Ink (*v.* OFFICE). *Inchiostro di china* is 'Indian ink' —and note that this doesn't mean, literally, 'Chinese ink', as China is *Cina* in Italian, and the corresponding adjective *cinese*.

incidente (m). The usual word for 'accident' (*v.* **accidente**).

indicatore (m). Indicator. *L'indicatore di direzione* is 'direction indicator' and *indicatore di velocità* is 'speedometer'.

indice (m). Index (*v.* OFFICE).

indifferente. When you really don't mind one way or the other, or else you politely wish to convey this impression, this is the word to use. 'Would you rather go to the Fiamma or the Fiammetta?'—'It's all the same to me', *Per me è indifferente*. It does not give the same impression of lack of interest as the English word.

indirizzo (m). Address, such as you write on the *busta* (f), the envelope.

indossatrice (f). Literally 'one (f) who puts (clothes) on', from the verb *indossare*, 'to put (clothes) on'. Actually here we are thinking of a model, a mannequin. *Modello* means 'model' in the sense of 'pattern' or 'design'.

infatti. 'In fact'. I have heard people saying that this form is just 'something you will find in the dictionary, but rarely used'. Don't you believe it. *Infatti* is used very frequently, and not least of all as the first word in a sentence which gives the idea, 'And, in fact, . . . '. And just as a point of interest, dictionaries do not normally give *infatti*, but rather *in fatto*, *di fatto*, *effettivamente*.

ingrassaggio (m). Greasing (*v.* CARS). 'Grease' is *grasso* and 'to grease' is *ingrassare*.

inizio (m). Put in here to remind you to use this word when you want to say 'beginning'. *L'inizio della lezione* is 'the start of the lesson'. *All'inizio* means 'at the beginning'. *L'inizio della strada* is 'the beginning of the road'. The verb *iniziare*, of course, is not the only verb with the meaning 'to begin'—there is also *cominciare*, for instance. A useful expression is *cominciare da capo*, 'to begin right from the very beginning (again)'.

in palio. At stake (*v.* SPORT). *Un palio* is 'a race' or else the 'race course'.

insalata (f). Salad (*v.* FOOD). Speaking of salad, the words involved here are *pomodoro* (tomato), *lattuga* (lettuce), *maionese* (f) (mayonnaise), *cetriolo* (cucumber) and *olio d'oliva* (olive oil).

inserire. To insert, to put in. *Inserire la spina* is 'to plug in', *i.e.* 'to put in the plug'. The plug is put into the socket, *presa* (f) *di corrente*.

insinuare. The meaning I want to emphasize here is 'to suggest', 'to hint'. *Cosa insinua?* is 'What are you hinting at?' To hint can also possibly be *alludere*, or even *accennare velatamente a qualche cosa*, but I prefer *insinuare*. *Capire a volo*, by the way, is 'to take a hint'.

insomma. One of those words put in to prop up a sentence, often with little or no meaning. Something like the English 'anyway'. Actually, the dictionary meanings of 'on the whole' and 'in short' are also often kept to. *Aveva la piega impeccabile ai calzoni, i guanti bianchi, l'ombrello nella mano, l'aria, insomma, di un uomo distinto*, 'He had impeccably creased trousers, white gloves, an umbrella in his hand, in short, the look of a distinguished man'. *In questo caso è la parola giusta, insomma*, means 'In this case it's the exact word, actually'. *Sì, è vero, ma non si dice, insomma* is 'Yes, it's true, but you don't say it, you see'. *La parola 'dai' si dice più che altro per incorraggiare un'altra persona, insomma, per farla cercare meglio, ecco*. This is 'The word "dai" is used more than anything else to encourage another person, that's to say, to make him try harder, you see'. *Sì, ma, insomma . . .* , 'Yes, but, anyway . . .'. *Ma insomma, che c'è?* 'But whatever is this?'

intendere. This is not the usual word for 'understand' (which is *capire*). I wish to stress only the expressions *s'intende* ('of course') and *per chi s'intende.* . . . ('for the one who understands these things, for the connoisseur' etc.). Note, too, the expression *Intendiamoci bene,* 'Let's get this quite straight', 'Let's put this point quite clearly', 'Don't let's misunderstand each other'.

interruttore (m). A switch. *Girare l'interruttore* is 'to turn the switch'. For 'to put on the light' *see* **luce.**

in vantaggio. 'Leading' (on points, by two to one, and so on) (*v.* SPORT).

invece. This may be either 'instead of' (when followed by *di*) or 'on the contrary', 'on the other hand'. You will hear it rather more than you might imagine, with the second meaning. For example, *Aveva l'intenzione di venire domani, ma è venuto oggi, invece* ('He intended to come tomorrow, but he's come today instead'). It often corresponds to the English 'though' at the end of a sentence, or to the word 'actually'. *Dopo aver promesso di fare tante cose, ha lasciato l'ufficio senza fare niente, invece,* 'After promising to do so many things, he left the office without actually doing anything'. *Lui dice che è molto urgente, ma io dico che non c'è urgenza, invece,* 'He says that it's very urgent, but I say there's no hurry, though'. *Bianchi ha giocato bene, ma Rossi invece ha giocato molto male,* 'Bianchi played well, but Rossi, on the other hand, played very badly'.

L

lampada (f). 'Lamp' or 'bulb'; *una lampadina* is 'a bulb' (*v.* HOUSEHOLD).

lampone (m). Raspberry. Nothing at all to do with being augmentative of *lampo,* which means 'lightning' or 'flash'. Notice that 'a zip fastener' is *una cerniera lampo.*

lana (f). Wool (*v.* HOUSEHOLD).

lanciare. To throw. The other word meaning 'to throw' is *gettare.* More precision or strength is sometimes implied in *lanciare,* as when it is used in sports, for instance.

lancio (m). A 'throw'. Notice the following sports names:
    lancio del disco, throwing the discus
    lancio del giavellotto, throwing the javelin
    lancio del martello, throwing the hammer
    lancio del peso, putting the shot
The one who throws is *un lanciatore.*

largo. A familiar false friend, meaning 'wide', as with the French *'large'*. The English 'large' is normally *grande*. There is also a noun, *un largo*, meaning variously 'width', 'largo' (in music), and 'square' (in the urban sense, such as *piazza*). A *largo* is usually wider than long, or longer than wide, as you will.

lasciare. 'To leave' or 'to let' (in the sense of 'allow'). Therefore, *lasciare* closely follows the meanings of the English 'leave'. *Lasciami stare* is 'Let me be'. *Lascia stare* is 'Leave it alone'. As in many languages, 'to drop' is put in the form of 'to let fall', *lasciare cadere*. *Lasciò cadere il giornale e tornò a passeggiare nel parco*, 'He dropped the paper and went on with his walk in the park'. Note particularly the idiomatic use of *lasciare perdere*, corresponding to the English 'Let it go at that', 'All right, we'll let that pass' and so on.

lastra (f). *Una lastra di vetro* is 'a window pane', 'a pane of glass' (v. HOUSEHOLD).

latte (m). Milk (v. FOOD). Note that the gender is masculine, as in French and differing from Spanish (*la leche*). *Latte condensato* is 'condensed milk'. In the summer, a popular drink in 'bars' is *latte di mandorla*, 'almond milk'.

latteria (f). Dairy (v. SHOPS).

lattuga (f). Lettuce (v. FOOD). As there are several sorts of lettuce, it is common to refer to the type rather than to refer to the generic word. Thus one often asks for a *cappuccina*.

laurea (f). An academic degree. To take one's degree is *prendere la laurea*, and the reflexive verb 'to obtain one's degree' is *laurearsi* (shall we be pessimistic and mention the verb 'to fail, to dip one's examination'? It is *essere bocciato*). The general word for passing an exam is *essere promosso*. *L'università dove si era laureato qualche anno prima* is 'The university where he had obtained his degree a few years earlier'. A *laureato* is a graduate of a university. Here are some examples of degrees:

> *Laureato in giurisprudenza*, B.L.
> *Laureato in ingegneria*, B.Sc. (Eng.)
> *Laureato in lettere*, B.A.
> *Laureato in medicina*, B.Med.
> *Laureato in scienze commerciali*, B.Com.

lavabo (m). Washbasin (v. HOUSEHOLD).

lavandino (m). Kitchen sink (v. HOUSEHOLD). Also 'washstand'.

lavare. To wash. 'To dry clean' is *lavare a secco*.

lavatrice (f). Washing machine (v. HOUSEHOLD).

legume (m). Vegetable (v. FOOD). *See also* **verdura.**

lenticchie (f pl). Lentils (v. FOOD).

lentiggine (f). 'Freckle'; and the adjective 'freckled' is *lentig-ginoso*. Quite straightforward, although dictionaries often complicate things by giving translations such as 'lentigo' and 'lentiginous'!

lenzuolo (m). Sheet (*v.* HOUSEHOLD). 'A sheet of paper' is *un foglio*.

letto (m). Bed (*v.* HOUSEHOLD). 'To go to bed' is *andare a letto* or alternatively *coricarsi*.

lettura (f). Not altogether straightforward, as it means 'reading', from the verb *leggere*, 'to read'. 'A lecture', on the other hand, is *una conferenza*.

leva (f). Lever (*v.* CARS). *Una leva liberacarta* is 'a paper release lever' (*v.* OFFICE).

libreria (f). A bookshop, not to be confused with 'a library', which is *una biblioteca* (although, apart from private ones, you will have to look hard to find one in Italy).

libro (m). Book. *Un libro di cassa* is 'a cash book', 'an account book' (*v.* OFFICE). The *libro paga* is the 'payroll'.

lì lì. 'On the point of', 'just about to'. *La ragazza era lì lì per piangere* means 'The girl was on the verge of tears'.

limone (m). Lemon (*v.* FOOD). The verb 'to squeeze' is *spremere*, and *una spremuta di limone* is 'a drink of lemon squash'.

lineetta (f). Dash (in the sense of an elongated hyphen) (*v.* OFFICE).

lingua (f). Tongue, both in the sense of the thing you have in your mouth, and (more so than in English) 'language'. You will probably have read somewhere the over-quoted refrain *Lingua toscana in bocca romana*. Well, Italians are not so familiar with this as some English books would have you believe, and at any rate they dispute its validity. *Lingua toscana*, yes, but *bocca romana*?

liquidazione (f). This, the dictionary tells you, may be 'clearance sale', which it is, or 'winding up' of a company, or 'liquidation', all equally correct. But the mention of the word brings another image to the mind of the average Italian. Under Italian law, a 'liquidation' is payable to an employee on the termination of his employment, if he has done a certain time with the firm. This 'liquidation' is calculated on the income received and the time worked, and is quite a hefty sum in some cases. We might call it the 'final settlement' or 'end-of-work bonus'.

liquido (m). Liquid. *Liquido per freni* is 'brake fluid' (*v.* CARS).

litigare. 'To quarrel.' This denotes one stage further than just *discutere* which, done *animatamente*, indicates some degree of raised voices. 'An altercation' or 'quarrel' is *un litigio* (or possibly *una disputa*).

logico. Logical. 'That's logical enough', you'll say. However, you would not normally say 'That's logical' anything like so many times as an Italian says *È logico*. The Italian often uses it to mean 'That's right' or 'Of course'. Quite often the point in question is not at all a logical one, but will be referred to as *logico*, just the same.

lombata (f), **lombo** (m). Sirloin (*v.* FOOD).

lotteria (f). A lottery. In Italy the lottery habit is not so widespread as in Spain. There are always lottery tickets being sold, but there's quite a long time from the first appearance of the tickets to the final draw. Small street kiosks house people selling the tickets, and towards the day for the draw you will read *Ultimi giorni*, and even later *Ultime ore*: but things are not always so imminent as they seem, as these *ultime ore* can stretch out for a few days.

lubrificatore (m). Lubricator (*v.* CARS).

lubrificazione (f). Lubrication (*v.* CARS).

luce (f). Light. 'To put the light on' is *accendere la luce*, and 'to put the light off' is *spegnere la luce*. *Una luce posteriore* is 'a rear light'. 'A fog light' is *una luce fendinebbia*.

lucidare. To polish. 'A floor polisher' is *una lucidatrice*; it is quite common in Italian homes, where there are so many floors made of marble-type stone.

lunetta (f). The rear window of a car (*v.* CARS).

lungomare (m). 'Promenade' in the sense of what you walk along by the sea. A promenade, in the sense of 'a stroll', is *una passeggiata*. If the promenade is along the banks of a river it is not a *lungomare* but a *lungo* plus 'name of river'. Rome, for instance, has the *Lungotevere*, the 'Along by the River Tiber'.

M

ma. *Ma* means 'but', of course, but it is used more in Italian than is 'but' in English. Apart from the fact that it is so often used alone accompanied by an expressive look and/or gesture, it is also used in the combinations *ma sì, ma no, ma che! ma che cosa?* (meaning respectively 'oh, yes, it is' etc., 'oh no, it's not, not at all, never' etc., 'what's all this?' 'you don't say' etc.)

macchina (f). Machine, obviously, and referring of course to whatever machine is specifically indicated, such as *macchina da scrivere*, meaning 'typewriter'. If there is a sewing-machine handy, then the *macchina* referred to will in all probability be the *macchina da cucire*. Similarly with *macchina stampa-indirizzi*, 'addressing machine', and so on. However, *una macchina* will nine times out of ten refer to a car, for which it is the sole colloquial word.

macelleria (f). Butcher's (*v.* SHOPS). The butcher himself is the *macellaio*.

macello (m). Although dictionaries will tell you truthfully that this means 'slaughterhouse', this is not half the story. Colloquially, in parts of Italy, and especially Rome, *macello* refers to any sort of 'shambles'. *Che macello!* 'What a mess!' 'What a shambles!' This can refer to the shambles someone makes of his work, or the shambles the children make of their playroom, or the shambles the cars make of the car park in wet weather, or the shambles politicians make of negotiations and so on.

magari. Why dictionaries don't say so I can't imagine, but *magari* has two clear meanings: 'perhaps' and 'if only'. Meaning 'perhaps', it is just about the same as *forse*, the usual dictionary word, while the other meaning is the same as the Spanish '*Ojalà!*' 'If only it were', 'I wish it were' etc. *Cosa faresti se avessi cento milioni lire?* 'What would you do if you had a hundred million lire?' *Magari!* 'I just wish I had!' Coming into contact with the Italian of everyday use after having studied from books outside Italy, this is one of the words most likely to strike you, as it crops up again and again.

magazzino (m). A false friend. It means 'store', 'large shop', and not at all the English magazine which you read, which is *rivista* in Italian.

maglia (f). Something knitted (and also 'stitch', 'mesh', according to context). *La maglia gialla*, 'the yellow vest' or 'yellow jersey', is the garment of honour worn by the cyclist leading (the overall position, including all stages) in the '*Tour de France*', *Il Giro di Francia*.

magnete (m). Magneto (*v.* CARS).

mai. This means 'never', of course, but it is also used in a number of circumstances when it cannot be a translation of 'never', but rather perhaps of 'ever'. *Non è mai troppo tardi*; this is regular and means 'It's never too late'. An expression you hear hundreds of times is *Come mai?* 'However . . . ?' 'How on earth?' *Come mai non ha finito il lavoro?* 'Why on earth haven't you finished the work?' *Ho visto che ha cancellato il suo nome—come mai?* 'I've noticed that you've crossed your name off—why on earth have you done this?'

    Mai più means 'never again', as you would expect. *Caso mai* is also used very many times, meaning 'Just in case'. *Non credo che possa chiederlo, ma caso mai lo lascio qui*, 'I don't think he'll ask for it, but just in case I'll leave it here'.

maiale (m). This may be either 'pig', the animal, or 'pork', the meat. And note that the place to go to buy pork chops is the *salsamenteria*, the grocer's, and not the butcher's.

male. This can be 'evil' or 'badly', with many variations, as you must know. Note that *Mi fa male* means 'It hurts me'. *Non c'è male* corresponds to our 'not so bad', when answering the question 'How are you?' The question *Che male c'è?* asks 'What's wrong with it?' When someone says *Sono rimasto molto male*, he means 'I was very disappointed'. *Meno male* (*q.v.*) means 'just as well', 'thank heavens' and so on, according to the occasion.

malincuore. 'To do something reluctantly' is *fare una cosa a malincuore*.

mamma mia! Whoever in English would say 'My mother!' as an exclamation? However, in Italian it is a common interjection, uttered in various tones according to the feeling. And Italians aren't necessarily content to say it just once. Some people repeat it to give added emphasis, or further outlet for the feelings.

mancanza (f). *Sentire la mancanza di qualcuno* means 'to miss someone'. *In mancanza di meglio* corresponds to the French '*faute de mieux*', or 'for want of something better'. Anyway, this word indicates the idea of lack, as in *mancanza di tempo*, 'lack of time'.

mancare. You will be well aware that the basic meaning of this verb is 'to be lacking'. *Manca un libro* means 'There is one book missing', for instance. *Ne mancano almeno cinque* means 'At least five are missing', or else 'We are short of five at least'. Another example: *Una notizia che, se non è sensazionale, per lo meno non manca di originalità*, 'Some news which, although perhaps not exactly sensational, is at least not lacking in originality'.

Non mancava che questo is the equivalent of 'This is the last straw'. Notice the construction *mancar poco* which means 'to come near to', 'to have nearly done something'. *Mi manca poco a concludere questo lavoro* means 'I'm very near to finishing this job'. *Poco mancò che fosse licenziato* is 'He came very near to being dismissed'.

In time expressions, *mancare* shows the number of minutes to the hour. *Mancano cinque minuti alle dieci* means 'It's five to ten'. When followed by the word *a*, *mancare* gives the idea of failure to do something. *Mancare a un appuntamento* means 'not to turn up for an appointment'. *Non mancare di fare qualche cosa* is 'not to fail to do something'. Used as a transitive verb, *mancare* means 'to miss' in the physical sense. One often hears a polite expression supplied by this verb, *Ci mancherebbe*. This means 'I don't want to put you out', or 'Please don't inconvenience yourself' and so on. *Ti accompagno alla fermata*, for instance, may have the reply *Ci mancherebbe*. This would be, more or less, 'I'll come with you to the (bus) stop', with the reply 'No, don't bother to do that'.

mancia (f). In a country where tipping is so widespread, this is an essential word. *Una mancia* is 'a tip', in the sense of 'a gratuity', as indicated. Otherwise 'a tip' can be *un consiglio*, 'a piece of advice'.

mandorla (f). Almond (*v.* FOOD).

mania (f). Remember the stress on the *i* of this word, which corresponds to the English 'craze'. *È proprio una mania* means 'It's a real craze'.

manico (m). Handle (of a cup or a tool, for example) (*v.* HOUSEHOLD).

maniglia (f). Handle. *Maniglia dello sportello* is 'door handle' (*v.* CARS).

mano (f). Need it be pointed out that it is *LA mano? Stringere la mano a . . .* is 'to shake hands with . . .'. *Mano mano*, or more commonly, *man mano*, means 'gradually, by degrees, taking it easy'. In painting (doors and windows and things like that, I mean), *una mano* refers to 'a coat of paint'.

manopola (f). Knob (*v.* HOUSEHOLD).

manovella (f). Crank (*v.* CARS). *La manovella alzacristallo* is 'the window handle'.

manubrio (m). Handlebars (*v.* SPORT).

manzo (m). Beef (*v.* FOOD).

maratona (f). Marathon (*v.* SPORT).

marcia (f). Walk, walking, as used in sport. *Marcia indietro* is 'reverse' (*v.* CARS).

marciapiede (m). Pavement. Note that *pavimento* is 'floor'. *Pavimento di legno* is a 'wooden floor'.

marinato. 'Pickled' (*v.* FOOD).

marmellata (f). 'Jam.' You could also call it 'marmalade', but this is a much more narrowly defined word in English than in Italian. Strictly speaking, in Italian 'marmalade' is *marmellata di arance*.

martello (m). 'Hammer.' This refers both to the tool and to the thing thrown in the sport called 'throwing the hammer', *lancio del martello*.

maschio (m). A male. A male child is *un maschio*, as opposed to a girl, who would be referred to as *una femmina* (*q.v.*) at birth.

massaggiatore (m). 'Masseur' (*v.* SPORT).

matita (f). 'Pencil' (*v.* OFFICE).

matto. 'Mad.' *Matto da legare* is 'stark, staring mad'. 'To drive someone round the bend' is *far diventare matto qualcuno*. The more formal word for a lunatic is *un folle*, but people use *un matto* or *un pazzo* (*q.v.*). Now quite another thing: in chess, the term 'checkmate' is *scacco matto*. The verb is *dare scacco matto*.

mattone (m). This is a 'brick', therefore something heavy, therefore, by extension, something boring.

mattonella (f). 'Floor tile' (v. HOUSEHOLD).

mediano (m). 'Half-back' (football) (v. SPORT).

mela (f). 'Apple.' *Melone* is 'melon' (v. FOOD).

meno. There are several expressions using this word. *Più o meno* means 'more or less', and is used as much as English speakers use this expression or Spaniards use *'más o menos'*. *Almeno* or *per lo meno* mean 'at least'. *A meno che. . .* means 'unless . . .'. *Vengo senz'altro, a meno che non ci sia qualcosa da fare urgentemente* is 'I'll come for sure, unless something has to be done urgently'. *Meno male* is one of the very most used expressions, meaning 'just as well', 'luckily', 'it's a good job', 'fortunately'. For example: *Piove ancora?*—No, ha smesso proprio adesso.— *Meno male, perchè non ho portato l'ombrello* ('Is it still raining?' —'No, it's just stopped.'—'A good job too, as I haven't brought an umbrella').

Fare a meno di . . . often means 'to do without something'. *Possiamo fare a meno di questo, mi pare* means 'We can do without this, I think'. When something cannot be helped or avoided, once again we have the word *meno*, as in this example: *Non ho potuto fare a meno di sentire quello che dicevate*, 'I couldn't help hearing what you were saying'.

menta (f). Mint (v. FOOD).

mente (f). 'Mind.' *Avere in mente* is 'to have in mind'. *Venire in mente* means 'to come to mind, to remember'. *Mi saltò in mente di fare così* means 'I got a sudden urge to do this'.

merciaio (m). Haberdasher, haberdasher's (v. SHOPS).

merluzzo (m). Cod (v. FOOD).

messaggero (m). 'Messenger.' The important thing to note is that one of the largest Italian daily papers is the Rome *'Messaggero'*. Thursdays and Sundays are the big days for advertisements, if you are looking for a room or a flat, or want to buy or sell something, and so on.

mettere. To put. *Mettere in testa* is 'to put an idea into someone's head'; *mettersi a fare qualche cosa* is 'to begin to do something'. Remember the use of the word where the English equivalent is 'to put plus preposition'. For example, *mettere la televisione*, which means 'to put the television on', *mettersi il cappello*, 'to put your hat on'. Note well the past participle *messo*. *La messa in marcia automatica* is 'the self-starter' of a car (v. CARS). Speaking of cars, *mettere in marcia* means 'to put in gear', and *mettere fuori marcia* is 'to put out of gear'.

metro (m). One metre, just as *metro quadrato* is a 'square metre'. It may also be a 'ruler' (wooden, one metre in length); *un metro a nastro* is 'a tape measure'.

metropolitana (f). The 'Tube' or 'Underground'. The Rome *Metropolitana* runs from the Central Station out to Ostia. Actually, only a part of its length is under ground, as it traverses a long stretch of country before coming to the seaside.

mezzo (m). 'Means.' *Un mezzo di trasporto* is 'a means of transport'. It may also mean 'half', or 'medium' (as in 'a medium of communication').

mica. This is an extremely common little word, used to give the idea of 'not at all', 'not in the slightest'. In answer to the question *Come sta?* one often hears the answer *Qui non c'è male*, or *Mica male*. That is to say 'Not so bad'. *Lei non è mica stupida* means that she is not at all stupid. *Mica capisce che senza di noi morirebbe di fame* means 'She doesn't understand at all that without us she would starve to death'.

midollo (m). Marrow (vegetable) (*v.* FOOD).

miele (m). Honey (*v.* FOOD). As in many languages, 'honeymoon' is *luna di miele*.

minestra (f). 'Soup.' *Minestrone* is also 'soup', but this time it is 'vegetable soup'. Remember that the Italians have several different words for 'soup'. There is also *brodo*, which really corresponds to our 'broth', and there is *zuppa*, which is the word usually used when the soup is qualified, as, for instance, *zuppa di piselli*, 'pea soup', or *zuppa di testuggine*, 'mock turtle soup'.

mobile (m). An article of furniture. You will see the word *Mobili* outside shops specializing in furniture (*v.* SHOPS).

modello (m). A bit of a false friend, as it refers to some sorts of models but not to all. It is specifically a pattern, or a miniature, as a model train. For the model who walks around with the latest fashions on, *see* **indossatrice**.

modo (m). 'Way' or 'manner'. *È il mio modo di parlare* means 'It's my manner of speaking'. Similarly, *modo di pensare*, 'way of thinking'. *Ognuno a suo modo* is 'Everyone in his own way'. *Fare una cosa in modo che ci sia un buon risultato* is 'to do something so that a good result is assured'. *Farò in modo di arrivare presto* means 'I'll arrange/manage to come early'. *In nessun modo* means 'not at all', 'in no way'. And the most important point of all here is that *in ogni modo* means 'anyway', 'at any rate', 'in any case'. For example: *Vengo dopo pranzo. Vengo in ogni modo prima delle cinque* ('I'll come after lunch. I'll be along before five at any rate'). *In ogni modo* is very useful to stick in, as an alternative to *comunque* (*q.v.*), where you would say 'anyway' in English.

molla (f). Spring (*v.* CARS).

momento (m). This means 'moment', of course. 'Wait a moment' may be translated *Aspetti* (or *attenda*) *un momento*, or else *Aspetti un attimo*. 'Just a moment' is often best rendered by

Un attimo solo. A common expression is *ad un certo momento*, to indicate that, at a certain point in one's narrative, something occurred. This is often simply 'then', possibly 'all at once', in English.

montone (m). Mutton (*v.* FOOD). This is in full *carne di montone*, *montone* being the animal, unlike the English.

mora (f). Blackberry (*v.* FOOD).

morire. To die. The infinitive is quite straightforward. *Morire di qualche cosa* is 'to die of something'. *Morire di fame* is 'to starve to death'. Less straightforward are the forms of the verb, such as *muoio* (I die) and so on, but you should be quite aware of such technicalities. *Quasi morto di sonno* means 'almost dead from lack of sleep', but the English somehow doesn't give the same idea as the Italian, as *morto di sonno*, and equally *morto di fame*, are common expressions not always referring just to the bare fact, but putting in a touch of irony, for example: *Eccolo che viene, morto di sonno*, 'Here he comes, and he can hardly keep his eyes open'.

Notice the expression *da morire*, corresponding to 'terribly so'. *Fa freddo?—Sì, da morire.*

motivo (m). 'Reason' or 'cause'. *Adesso ha un motivo di più per fare così*, 'Now he has yet another reason to do that'. *Per quale motivo?* means 'For what reason, on what grounds?'

motociclo (m). Motor-bike (*v.* CARS). The sport of 'motorcycling' is called *motociclismo*.

motore (m). 'Motor' or 'engine'. *Motore a benzina* is 'petrol engine'. *Un motore a comando diretto* is 'a direct-drive axle motor'. *Motore a combustione interna* is 'internal combustion engine'. The English 'straight eight' is *motore ad otto cilindri in linea* and the 'flat twin' is *motore a due cilindri contrapposti*. A 'two-stroke engine' is *motore a due tempi*. 'A jet engine' is *un motore a getto*; 'jet-propelled' would be *con motore a getto*.

Notice that *una motoretta* is 'a motor scooter', and that a 'motorboat' is *motoscafo*. The word *motorista* is a false friend, as it means 'engineer' rather than 'motorist', as in *motorista di bordo*, 'flight engineer'.

mozzarella (f). Mozzarella cheese, sold in shiny white balls, and sometimes made from buffalo milk, *mozzarella di bufala*. This cheese is used in cooking, in rice-balls, for example, and can be drawn out to great lengths like chewing gum.

mozzicone (m). Although this may refer to a 'stump' or 'broken piece' in general, it in fact refers almost exclusively to a 'fag-end' or 'cigarette-end'. The other slight possibility is that it may refer to a lump of bread, *un mozzicone di pane*, although *tozzo* is more often used in this context. *Guadagnarsi un tozzo di pane* means 'to scrape a living together', 'to struggle to make ends meet', 'to struggle for a crust', or just plain 'to earn one's living'.

mozzo (m). 'Hub' (*v.* CARS). *Mozzo del disco della frizione* is 'clutch disc hub'. On board ship, *mozzo* refers to the 'cabin boy'.

mucchio (m). 'Heap' or 'pile'. This is a current expression for 'a lot of'. *Guadagna un mucchio di soldi* means 'He earns a heck of a lot of money'. *Stamane ho ricevuto un mucchio di lettere*, 'I got a whole heap of letters this morning'.

N

nascosto. *Fare una cosa di nascosto* means 'to do something on the sly'.

nastro (m). 'Tape' or 'ribbon', and even 'strap' or 'band'. On a typewriter it is the 'typewriter ribbon'. *Nastro isolante* is 'insulating tape'. *Un nastro metrico* is 'a tape-measure'.

nazionale (m). The sportsman of this variety is what we refer to as an 'international'. The Italians in their sports papers more often than not refer to him (if he is Italian) as *un azzurro*, 'a blue'. *Nazionale* in a grocer's shop (*salsamenteria*) would be cheese, home-produced Gruyère, in fact.

ne. You should get it quite straight that while *ci* gives the basic idea of 'there' (place you are going to), as in *Ci vado domani*, 'I'm going there tomorrow', *ne* gives the idea of 'from here' or 'from there'. *Me ne vado* is 'I'm going' (from here, of course). You say *Vattene via* to order someone to 'Go away'. Note the use of both *ci* and *ne* in the following: *Ci sono stato l'anno scorso, per un mese. Ne sono partito solo quando non avevo più soldi.*

Naturally, this by no means exhausts the possibilities of *ne*. We have 'of it', 'about it', 'some', 'them' and so on, as you will have studied.

negozio (m). Shop (*see also* **bottega**). The girl assistant is called *una commessa*. Note that a large store is *un magazzino*, while *una ditta* corresponds to 'a firm'.

nero. Black, as you well know. Another colour to add to the collection of those with subsidiary meanings (*see* **verde, giallo** and **azzurro**). Referring to someone's mood, when we say *È piuttosto nero questa mattina*, we mean 'He's in a bit of a bad mood this morning'. *Nero di avorio* is 'ivory black'. In Italian football, *i neroverdi* is the name applied to the First Division team of *Atalanta* (*v.* SPORT).

nettapiedi (m). Floor mat (*v.* HOUSEHOLD).

niente. There are a few expressions to be emphasized here. *Non c'è niente da fare* means 'There's nothing that can be done'. (More about this later.) *Di niente* is the polite answer to make if someone thanks you: *Grazie mille.*—*Di niente* ('Thank you very much'. 'Don't mention it'). Or you could use *Ci mancherebbe* (*q.v.*) or, of course, *prego* (*q.v.*). *Non fa niente* means 'It doesn't matter', 'It's quite all right'. *Non sa nuotare per niente* shows the use of *per niente* to stress the negative. In this case the meaning is: 'He can't swim for toffee', 'He hasn't got the first idea of how to swim'. *Lei non è intelligente per niente* means 'She isn't at all intelligent'.

Niente da fare, as indicated, means 'There's nothing you can do', 'There's nothing that can be done' and so on. Said perhaps with a shrug of the shoulders. If you ask a taxi-driver to get you somewhere quickly at the rush hour, avoiding the traffic, he'll probably do his best, but he'll not be able to avoid all the jams, and apart from his curses he'll tell you *Non c'è niente da fare*. This is one of the two vocabulary indications of acceptance of things as they are. The other one, the more submissive one, is the often-used *pazienza* (*q.v.*). Both expressions give an idea of one's being unable to change things, however wrong they may be. After a long wait in the 'queue' at the registry office (*anagrafe*), for example, a man might be told that he had all his documents in order except for one signature on the last Birth Certificate, perhaps ten years old. And without this, the clerk will explain, *Non c'è niente da fare. Ci vuole assolutamente la firma* ('It's indispensable to have the signature'). And the poor chap, not being able to claim family allowances yet, may well collect up his papers and mutter *Pazienza!*

nocciola (f). Hazel nut (*v.* FOOD). *Noccioline* are 'peanuts'.

noce (f). Nut (*v.* FOOD). *Noce moscata* is 'nutmeg'. *Noce* is also 'walnut'.

noioso. Nothing to do with 'noisy', but with boredom. *Noioso* is 'boring' (*see also* **seccante** and **scocciante**). 'Noisy' is *rumoroso* or *chiassoso*.

non so. As you know, this means 'I don't know'. Rather elementary, you'll no doubt be thinking. Are you one of those people who are always putting in 'I don't know' in English sentences? Many speakers of all languages do this, you know, usually not realizing it and certainly hardly ever willing to recognize the fact. Well, in Italian you'll often hear *non so* said. Sometimes at the beginning of, sometimes inside and sometimes at the end of sentences. It's one of those 'prop' expressions, to support an unbalanced sentence, to put an end to an unfinished one, to let you out of finding the '*mot juste*', or even a fairly suitable word or expression. In Italian, the users of *non so* are usually those who use also *come si chiama?* and *coso* (*q.v.*). 'I don't know—what d'you call it?—what's its name?' and so on.

L'altro giorno stavo parlando con coso, come si chiama?—il fratello di coso—sì, Enzo, giusto. Allora, non so, mi disse che non voleva che—come si chiama?—Enzo, facesse così. Io, non so, non voglio mai litigare, ma in questo caso non ho potuto accettare, non so, e . . . etc, etc. Admittedly, this is stretching the point a bit, and certainly not to be recommended, but believe me, those who speak like this are more numerous than you might have imagined.

notorietà (f). 'Fame' or 'notoriety'. This Italian word does not of necessity have the same bad sense as the English cognate. If a person has a certain *notorietà* he is not necessarily notorious in the English sense. Likewise with the adjective *notorio*, which means 'noted', 'famous', 'famed' or else 'notorious'. Otherwise 'famous' is of course *famoso*, and 'known', 'noted' is *conosciuto* (from the verb *conoscere*, which also gives *conoscente* (m or f), meaning 'acquaintance'. Another way to say that you have an acquaintance is *È qualcuno di mia conoscenza*, 'He is an acquaintance of mine').

novità (f). A piece of news. *Vuole sapere una novità?* 'Would you like to hear the latest news?' *Novità* always has this idea of 'the latest news', while *notizia* (f) is the ordinary word for 'piece of news' otherwise.

nulla (f). Nothing. *Non fa nulla* means 'It doesn't matter'. The meaning of *nulla* corresponds to that of *niente* (*q.v.*).

nuotare. To swim (*v.* SPORT). A swimmer is *un nuotatore*, and the sport or recreation itself is *il nuoto*. A swimming-pool is *una piscina*, and 'to dive' is *tuffarsi*.

O

oca (f). Goose.

occhiata (f). This is a 'glance'. *Dare un'occhiata* would be 'to have a glance at' or even 'to have a squint at'. The preposition following is *a*.

occorrere. Surprisingly, this verb means 'to be necessary', while the verb 'to occur' is *succedere* or *accadere*. *Non occorre aggiungere altro per dire che il confronto è stato mediocre* means 'It's not necessary to add anything else to say that the match was a mediocre one'. *Occorre farlo* is 'It has to be done'. *Mi occorrono mille lire* is 'I need a thousand lire'.

oculista (m). Oculist (*v.* SHOPS).

oh Dio (mio)! You will very often hear this exclamation. *Oh Dio, che cosa ho fatto?* It corresponds to 'Good heavens', 'My goodness' and so on. Often repeated, sometimes more than twice together. *Oh Dio, oh Dio!*

oliatore (m). Oil-can (*v.* CARS).

olio (m). Oil. *Olio d'oliva* is 'olive oil' (*v.* FOOD). *Olio lubrificante* is 'lubricating oil' (*v.* CARS). 'Whale oil' is *olio di balena*.

'Coconut oil' is *olio di cocco*. We mustn't omit 'cod liver oil', which is *olio di fegato di merluzzo*. *Olio di lino* is 'linseed oil'. *Olio di ricino* is 'castor oil'.

oliva (f). Olive (*v.* FOOD). 'Olive oil' is *olio d'oliva*. The 'olive tree' is the *olivo*—it is, of course, the rule that the tree in Italian has the same name as the fruit, apart from the fact that the fruit normally ends in *a*, while the tree ends in *o*. *Mela* (f) is 'apple', while *melo* is 'apple-tree'.

omaggio (m). The dictionary definition of 'homage' doesn't go very far towards helping us here. You will see the word quite often, for example, on a soap-powder packet. *Omaggio* is in fact used to mean 'free gift', and on the soap-powder packet it corresponds to our 'free gift inside'. A book presented by the author to someone will have the words *omaggio dell'autore* written inside, 'presented by the author'.

oppure. An alternative to just saying *o*, 'or'. Sometimes such a short word as *o* seems inadequate, as we feel in English with the word 'or' in some circumstances, because we often tack on the word 'else' to help out. So in Italian we have *oppure* instead of *o*. *Vengo alle cinque. Oppure, se no, vengo alle nove, dopo cena*, 'I'll come at 5, or else, if I don't, I'll come at 9, after supper'. *Si può dire: dodici oppure una dozzina*, 'You can say either 12 or else a dozen'.

orario (m). Time-table. *Orario di ufficio* is 'office hours' (*v.* OFFICE).

ordinario. Be a little careful in using this adjective. The word which most often corresponds to the English 'ordinary' is *normale*. The Italian word is usually best translated by 'common' or 'vulgar'.

orologeria (f). Watchmaker's, jeweller's (*v.* SHOPS). It is precisely the former word, of course, but can sometimes apply better to the latter, when all sorts of silver and other things are sold.

ostacoli (m pl). Hurdles, in running (*v.* SPORT). *400 ost.* is the usual newspaper manner of referring to the '400 metres hurdles'.

ostrica (f). Oyster (*v.* FOOD).

P

padella (f). Frying-pan (*v.* HOUSEHOLD).

pala (f). Shovel (*v.* HOUSEHOLD).

palazzo (m). This can be a 'palace', as you might conclude, but in everyday city talk it refers to a 'block of flats'. In fact, any large building divided up into many rooms will be referred to as a *palazzo*. Bear in mind that it need not necessarily be a fine building. The person in charge of the smooth running of the block, 'the porter' or '*concierge*', is called *il portinaio* (*q.v.*).

palestra (f). Gymnasium. The Italian *ginnasio* (*q.v.*) is an old false friend.

palla (f). Ball (*v.* SPORT). *Pallone* is also used for a bigger ball. *Pallacanestro* is 'basketball', a popular sport in Italy, and *pallanuoto* is 'water-polo'.

pane (m). Bread. *Un pezzo di pane* is 'a piece of bread'. *Una briciola* is 'a crumb'; *pangrattato* refers to 'breadcrumbs' in quantity, such as you buy to dip fish in before frying it. The expression *guadagnarsi un tozzo di pane* means 'to earn one's living', but stresses the difficulty of making ends meet.

panificio (m). The shop where you buy bread, the 'baker's'. Sometimes also called the *panetteria*.

panna (f). Cream (*v.* FOOD). Speaking of motor vehicles, *una panna* is a Gallicism for 'breakdown'. You say also, and with greater purity of language, *un guasto*, for this breakdown.

parabrezza (f). Windscreen (*v.* CARS). *Parafango* (m) is 'mudguard'. Still on the subject of cars, *parasole* is the 'sunscreen', and *paraurti* is the 'bumper'. *Il paraurti posteriore* is 'the rear bumpers'.

paragone (m). A standard of comparison. *Prendiamo l'anno 1954 come paragone* means 'Let's take 1954 as our base year'. *A paragone di . . .* means 'compared with . . . '. The English 'paragon' meaning 'ideal model' is best translated *modello perfetto*. For models, *see also* **modello**.

paragrafo (m). Paragraph (*v.* OFFICE).

parcheggiare. To park (*v.* CARS). The place to park, the 'car park', is called *parcheggio* (m). Nowadays perhaps you will find a 'parking meter' there, and this is *parcometro* in Italian. The chap there looking after the cars is the *custode* (m).

parecchio. 'Quite a lot', 'a good deal'. *Ha bevuto parecchio* means 'He has drunk quite a lot', *i.e.* 'He's a bit tight'. *C'è ancora parecchio da fare* is 'There's still quite a bit to do'. The masculine plural form is *parecchi*, and the feminine plural, *parecchie*. *Parecchie persone dicono che . . .* means 'Many people say that . . . '. You will find that this word is used *parecchio*, 'a good deal'.

pareggio (m). Draw or perhaps 'tie', in sport (*v.* SPORT). *See also* **parità** which is sometimes used (*un risultato di parità*). The verb 'to draw' is *pareggiare*.

parentesi (f pl). Brackets (*v.* OFFICE).

parmigiano (m). Parmesan cheese (*v.* FOOD).

parolaccia (f). The ending of this word shows that it refers to a crude word. It is, in fact, a 'bad word'. The plural *parolacce* means 'bad language', 'bad words'. *Mannaggia* is a mild example of a *parolaccia*, meaning 'curse it' etc.

parrucchiere (m). Hairdresser's (*v*. SHOPS).

partita (f). Game or match (*v*. SPORT). A boxing match will more likely be called *un incontro*. The word 'departure' is best rendered as *partenza* (f).

passaggio (m). Passage. *Passaggio a livello* is 'level crossing' (*v*. CARS). *Dare un passaggio* means 'to give a lift'.

passaporto (m). I mention this word, 'passport', as so many learners get the gender wrong. *Porto* is 'port', of the harbour variety, while *porta*, as you well know, is 'door'.

passerino (m). Plaice (*v*. FOOD).

pastasciutta (f). *Pasta*, apart from meaning 'fancy cake', is the word for 'dough', and *pastasciutta*, although the dictionary fails to inform you, is the staple Italian food of 'dried pasta', the generic term covering the myriad forms of what we generally refer to as 'spaghetti'. *Spaghetti* is in fact one sort, which should be too familiar to you for me to have to describe it. Perhaps the most generally popular type of all is *fettuccine*, fairly wide strips of *pasta*. *Cannelloni* are large-bore macaroni, and . . . but the list could go on to include literally dozens and dozens of shapes and sizes, from the smallest little star-shapes up to the largest shell-shapes, from the most fragile-looking threads up to the biggest *cannelloni*.

pasticcio (m). 'Pie.' But people using this word are not usually referring to pies. The main connotation of this word is of something in confusion, all messed up. *Che pasticcio!* means 'What a mess!' A *pasticcione* is a person who messes things up. If you say: *Tu sei un grande pasticcione* to someone, you are as good as saying "Trust you to muck things up". The sense of the word *pasticcio* corresponds to that of *guaio* (*q.v.*). You can say *essere nei pasticci* and *essere nei guai*, the former expression meaning rather that the person in question is 'in a bit of a mess, in trouble', while the latter expression means that there is perhaps 'real trouble', a really embarrassing or unfortunate predicament. However, I shouldn't like to make too much of this difference, as the force of the meaning depends more on the tone of the voice and on the exact form of the sentence, and even more on the personal choice of the speaker. Still, perhaps we could say that *pasticcio* is relatively light-hearted compared to *guaio*. *Pasticceria* can be the 'pastrycook's shop' (*i.e.* 'cake-shop') or the goods themselves (*una pasta* is used to denote a small cake, and *torta* a larger one that has to be cut up). The 'pastrycook' is the *pasticciere*. A recent newspaper report spoke of the illegal business carried on by a pastrycook in a southern Italian city, and the report ended by saying that *Il pasticciere si trova, adesso, nei pasticci.* He got four years.

pastinaca (f). Parsnip (*v.* FOOD).

pasto (m). Meal (*v.* FOOD). *Antipasto* is 'Hors d'œuvres'.

patata (f). Potato (*v.* FOOD).

patente (f). This is a licence, referring normally to 'a driving licence', which is fully *una patente di guida*. *Prendere la patente* is 'to take one's driving test'. The English 'patent' is *brevetto*.

pattumiera (f). Dustbin (*v.* HOUSEHOLD). Otherwise called the *secchio delle immondizie*, the 'rubbish bucket'. The 'dustpan' is called *porta-immondizie*.

pavimento (m). A common false friend. This word refers to the floor, while 'pavement' is *marciapiede* (m).

pazienza (f). As pointed out under *niente da fare*, this word gives the submissive idea of 'Oh, well, that's the way it is', 'It's no good complaining', 'Can't be helped, I suppose' and so on. Too frequent a use of it indicates overmuch submissiveness, but in small doses it's not a bad corrective to trying to batter down a brick wall, to do the impossible, that is. Children are often advised to have *pazienza*, when getting into a bit of a temper over something. In dealing with officialdom it is a necessary attribute.

pazzo (m). As mentioned under *matto* (*q.v.*), this is used for 'mad', 'insane' and so on. The person is *un pazzo* or *una pazza*, and 'madness' is *la pazzia*. *Sono pazzo del formaggio groviera* means 'I'm mad on Gruyère cheese'.

pedale (m). Pedal (*v.* CARS).

pelletteria (f). Skins in general, or rather things made of them, 'leather goods', are sold in the shop bearing this sign (*insegna*).

pellicciaio (m). Furrier (*v.* SHOPS).

pelo (m). 'Hair' in the sense of 'one strand of hair'. Do not use the word in the Spanish sense of 'your hair is black', for instance. The hair of your head is *i capelli*, definitely plural. And notice the other pitfall, that of spelling and pronunciation, which is caused by the existence of the word *cappello*, 'hat'. So *capelli* means 'hair/s', and *cappelli* 'hats', mind you!
      Notice also the expression *essere a un pelo di . . .* , 'to be within an ace of . . .', 'on the point of . . .'.   *Stava a un pelo di perdere la vita*, 'He was within an ace of losing his life'.

pendaglio (m). Strap-handle (*v.* CARS).

pennino (m). Pen nib (*v.* OFFICE).

pensione (f). Boarding-house. Some of the superior ones couldn't be called anything but 'hotels' in English (*v.* SHOPS).

pentola (f). Pot (*v.* HOUSEHOLD). *Pentola con rubinetto* is 'kettle'.

pepe (m). Pepper (*v.* FOOD). *Pepe bianco* is 'white pepper'.

pera (f). Pear (*v.* FOOD).

perchè. I mention this simple and fundamental word to remind you that it is used not only for 'why?' and for 'because', but also in the following way: *La ragazza implorava la madre perchè le desse una bambola.* 'The girl begged her mother to give her a doll'. Here the word *perchè* is the equivalent of *affinchè*. Note the subjunctive afterwards.

pericolo (m). Danger. *Correre un pericolo* is 'to run a risk'. The verb 'to endanger' is *mettere in pericolo*.

permesso (m). You should know all about this word meaning 'permission', 'leave', and so forth. The important thing to remember is that this is the word to say when you wish someone to move aside to let you go past: 'Excuse me, please'.

pernice (f). Partridge (*v.* FOOD).

però. Spanish speakers, note the accent at the end of the word, and also that 'but' ('*pero*' in Spanish) is *ma* ('*mas*' is the Spanish cognate), while *però* means 'however', 'yet'. You would not need to be told that the Italian unaccented *pero* is a 'pear-tree', I hope. *Sì, mi pare che lei potrebbe farlo,* 'Yes, I think you'd be able to do it'. *È difficile, però,* 'But it's difficult, mind'.

pesca (f). Peach (*v.* FOOD).

pesce (m). Fish (*v.* FOOD).

peso (m). Weight. In athletics, 'shot' (*v.* SPORT). *Un inglese ha migliorato oggi il proprio primato europeo di lancio del peso* means 'An Englishman has today improved his own European record for putting the shot'. The various boxing weights are as follows: *gallo,* 'bantam'; *leggero,* 'light'; *medio,* 'middle'; *mediomassimo,* 'light-heavyweight'; *massimo,* 'heavy'; *mosca,* fly'; *piuma,* 'feather'; *welters,* 'welter'.

pezzo (m). This is the usual word for 'piece' or 'bit'. *Un pezzo di carta* is 'a piece of paper' (otherwise, 'a sheet of paper' is *un foglio*). There are, however, two common usages of the word which deserve to be mentioned. *Un pezzo grosso* is 'an important person', 'a V.I.P.'. The other meaning refers to time. *Da un pezzo non la vedevo così allegra* means 'I had not seen her looking so gay for quite a long time'. *Già da un pezzo era giorno* is 'It had already been light for some time'.

piacere (m). Quite apart from the idea of pleasure, of which you are well aware, *piacere* is the word to use for 'a favour'. *Mi fa un piacere?* is 'Would you do me a favour?' *Per piacere* is 'please', and is used quite frequently. And remember that *piacere* is the word which corresponds to 'How do you do?' when being introduced (*presentato*) to someone. You say *piacere,* and he says *piacere,* and then, when you take your leave, you say *piacere* again.

piantare. The familiar use of this word is in the sense of 'to leave in the lurch', 'to leave holding the baby'. *Piantare grane* is 'to make trouble'. If told to *piantarla—piantala subito!* you are being exhorted to 'cut it out!'

piatto (m). Plate, dish (*v.* HOUSEHOLD). *Un piattino* is 'a saucer'.

piccarsi. This reflexive verb means 'to pride oneself on . . . '. *Lui che si picca di essere un discreto nuotatore* means 'He, quite a swimmer in his own opinion . . . ', or perhaps 'He, who prides himself on being a bit of a swimmer . . . '.

piccione (m). Pigeon (*v.* FOOD). Not to be confused with *pigione* (*q.v.*).

pigione (f). Nothing to do with birds (the pigeon is, as mentioned above, *il piccione*). No, this is what you have to pay for your room, flat, house etc., namely 'the rent'. You can also say *l'affitto*, but *pigione* is rather more popular.

pigliare. To take, to take to, to get into. *Pigliare fuoco* is 'to catch fire'. *Pigliare qualche cosa in buona parte* is 'to take something in good part'. Other meanings include 'to catch', 'to seize', 'to arrest', 'to cheat' and 'to deceive'. Remember the saying *Chi dorme non piglia pesci*, *viz.* 'The early bird catches the worm' (putting it positively). *Si sforzava di pigliare la vita come prima* means 'He tried hard to take life as he had before'. Remembering the multiplicity of meanings of *pigliare* (and the reflexive form *pigliarsi*), you will realize that it is not easy to give a definite translation. However, in current usage it is not a verb used with any great frequency.

pignolo. 'Fussy', in the sense of being a hair-splitter. About the same as 'pedantic'. *È troppo pignolo* is 'He's much too fussy'.

pinze (f pl). Pliers (*v.* HOUSEHOLD and CARS).

pisello (m). Pea (*v.* FOOD).

pista (m). Track (*v.* SPORT).

più che altro. This means 'mainly', 'chiefly', 'on the whole', 'as a rule'.

piuttosto. 'Rather' or 'quite'. *Era piuttosto grassa*, 'She was rather plump'. *Fa piuttosto caldo*, 'It's rather hot'.

pneumatico (m). Tyre (*v.* CARS). If you say *copertone* you are referring to the outer cover only, while the *pneumatico* is more the whole thing, outer cover and inner tube together.

poco (m). A little. In the plural, 'few'. *Conosco poche persone*, 'I know very few people'. *Poco fa* means 'a short time ago', while *fra poco* means 'in a short while'. *Lui è poco serio* is 'He is not very serious'. The reason for including this simple word here is that it is so often used, in a shortened form, in colloquial Italian, to give the meaning 'Just (do this)'. *Senta un po'* means 'Just listen to this'. *Dimmi un po'* is 'Just tell me'. Notice also that in saying 'a little bit of something', the

Italian is *un po' di* . . . , as in this example: *Vado a comprare un po' di carne*, 'I'm going to buy a little meat'.

poi. As you know, this is the word for 'then' in the sense of 'after that'. 'Then', the past of 'now', is of course *allora*. *Poi* is the word to shoot in when recounting a story and so on. ' . . . and then . . . '. When someone else is telling a story, and breaks off part way through, you may say *E poi?* where you might also say 'And then?' in English. Notice: *d'ora in poi*, 'from now on'; *da domani in poi*, 'from tomorrow onwards'; *prima o poi*, 'sooner or later'.

If you go shopping in Italy, in a grocer's shop, for example, after each item you ask for, the shopkeeper or assistant may very well say *Poi?* hoping for you to continue ordering things.

poliziotto (m). 'Policeman', 'police constable'. And this brings up the question—just what is the *polizia*, the police? I mean, there seem to be so many different kinds of them. The clear-cut ones, as it were, are the soldier type, the elegant *carabinieri*, who on special days parade or patrol in their red-striped and tailed uniform. They are of no uncertain pedigree, as they have to present details of several generations back, unstained and untarnished, when seeking entry. In fact, they are a branch of the military forces, and correspond very much to the Spanish *Guardia Civil*. However, although these catch the eye, they are not the ones who immediately conjure up the word 'policeman' when you catch sight of them. As a matter of fact, the most 'policeman'-looking sort are, without doubt, the spotless and very efficient traffic policemen. They very much resemble English policemen in the cooler months, with their blue uniforms and helmets. In the summer they have white boots and uniforms and helmets—and they really are white. These policemen are, however, concerned solely with traffic, and they certainly do not perform the all-round functions of their English counterparts. In fact, most of these functions are carried out by the 'cops', the *agenti*, the *agenti di pubblica sicurezza*, who wear flat-topped caps. The Riot Squads patrol in red jeeps marked *Celere* ('fast'). Motor-cycle patrolmen, *vigili*, their cycles marked *Polizia Stradale* (or else *Carabinieri*, if such they are) are much in evidence along certain roads, and particularly at certain periods, such as *Ferragosto* (*q.v.*). Also there are the *guardie di finanza* or *finanzieri*, the 'customs police', who guard many city buildings, apart from being busy along Italian frontiers and at ports. Two more notes: the municipal *metropolitani* have varied functions and may often be seen sporting armbands informing you of the foreign language they have command of. And, lastly, the ones who most resemble our ideas of what armed police should be are the members of the *Vigilanza Notturna*—slightly superior night-watchmen.

pollo (m). Chicken (*v.* FOOD).

poltrona (f). Although this can possibly mean a female poltroon
or lazy thing, it usually refers to an 'easy chair' or 'armchair'.
In a cinema you sometimes see the word *poltrona* in connexion
with the more comfortable seats to be occupied. In a sports
paper, an article is entitled *Poltrona di ring*, 'Ringside seat'.

pomodoro (m). Tomato (*v.* FOOD). *Salsa di pomodoro* is 'tomato
sauce' or 'ketchup'.

pompa (f). Pump (*v.* CARS). *Pompare* is the verb 'to pump'.

porcheria (f). 'Filth', 'dirt', 'dirty trick', 'lousy trick'. This is the
word that would be used in the Italian equivalent of the English
'What a filthy trick!' *Che porcheria!*

porro (m). Leek (*v.* FOOD).

portabagagli (m). Luggage rack, boot (*v.* CARS).

portacenere (m). Ashtray (*v.* HOUSEHOLD).

portalampada (m). Bulb socket (*v.* HOUSEHOLD).

portare. Naturally, the difficulty here is for Italian learners of
English, when they have to decide which verb to choose—
to bring, to carry, to bear, to wear and so on. One expression
you hear often in Italy is *portare fortuna*, 'to bring good luck'.

portiere (m). Goalkeeper (*v.* SPORT). *La portiera* is not the female
goalkeeper, but one of the names for the '*concierge*'.

portinaio (m). Door-keeper, porter, concierge. The lady in
charge of the block of flats, for example, is *la portinaia* or *la
portiera*. The room occupied by the concierge is known as
la portineria.

posto (m). Place, or 'room' in the sense of 'place'. *Non c'è posto*
means 'There isn't any room'. The word is used in a very
general sense. A police-station may be *un posto di polizia*,
and a fire-station *posto di pompieri*. 'On the spot' is *sul posto*.
Mettere tutto a posto means 'to put everything in order', 'to
put things straight'. It may also mean 'post' in the sense of
'employment'. *Ho trovato un posto magnifico*, 'I've found a
wonderful job'.

potenza (f). Power. Regarding cars, etc., it is 'horse-power'. *La
potenza marittima* is 'sea-power'.

pranzo (m). Dinner. The verb is *pranzare* (*v.* FOOD).

pratica (f). Folder, file (*v.* OFFICE).

praticamente. This adverb corresponds to the English 'practically' or 'in practice'. You will hear it used very often—not in
the sense of the English 'I've practically finished', where the
meaning is 'very nearly' and the Italian is *quasi*, but more
with the idea of 'in actual fact'.

prego. You absolutely must get into the *prego* habit. You say it
to someone who thanks you—'Don't mention it'. You say it to

let someone go past you, to give up your seat to someone, when handing someone something, in short, when doing someone a service with a smile. *Ve ne prego* is 'I beg you'. TV announcers, when at a live show, use *Ve ne prego* to attempt to calm noisy audiences. 'Ladies and gentlemen, please . . . '.

prendere. Just a short note on a verb of very varied application. In fact, more extensive notes are made unnecessary by there usually being such copious entries in the dictionary. 'To note' may be *notare*, but when it is a case of writing things down, you had better use *prendere appunti*. *Prendere il posto di* . . . is 'to replace . . . '. *Prendere qualcosa in prestita* means 'to borrow something'. *Vado a prendere un bicchiere* means 'I'm going to get a glass'. *Che cosa gli prende?* could be translated more or less as 'What's eating him?' 'What's got into him?' *Prendere in giro* is 'to pull someone's leg'.

preoccupare. 'To worry, preoccupy, make anxious'. Most often used reflexively, *preoccuparsi*, meaning 'to worry, be anxious, be worried'. *Non ti preoccupare* means 'Don't worry', 'Don't let it trouble you' and so on. The corresponding noun is *preoccupazione*, 'anxiety', 'worry'.

prepotente. This adjective is of much more frequent use than the dictionary equivalent, 'overbearing'. The noun *prepotenza*, 'overbearingness', as it were, is also common. *Fare il prepotente* is roughly 'to be too big for one's boots'. *È molto prepotente* therefore often means 'He's got too big an opinion of himself'. Speaking of a young child, the idea becomes more 'She's very forward for her age, isn't she?' or perhaps, 'He's not the slightest bit shy, is he?'

presa (f). Socket (*v.* HOUSEHOLD). *Presa diretta* is 'top gear' (*v.* CARS).

press'a poco. *Le strade sono due, e la lunghezza è press'a poco la stessa.* This means 'There are two roads, of about equal length'. *Press'a poco* is a common way of saying 'approximately'. 'Aproximately' may also be *circa* more often used with a number, which it follows. *Ho vinto cinque mila lire circa* means 'I've won about five thousand lire'.

preventivo (m). The word for 'estimate'. 'Prevention', of the sort which is better than cure, is rather *impedimento*.

prevenuto. This is a good word to use to say 'prejudiced', which somehow always seems difficult in a foreign language. *È sempre stato prevenuto contro mia famiglia* means 'He has always been prejudiced against my family'.

prezzemolo (m). Parsley (*v.* FOOD).

prima colazione (f). Breakfast (*v.* FOOD). Sometimes simply *la colazione.*

primato (m). Record, of the sort which is broken in sport. *Giorgio Rossi ha migliorato il primato mondiale di lancio del giavellotto* means 'George Rossi has improved on the world record for the javelin throw'. The record played by the disc jockey is, of course, *un disco*.

procurare. An example of an Italian verb which sounds stilted, or even immoral, to the English ear, but which is a common enough Italian equivalent of another English verb, in this case 'to get', in the sense of 'to obtain', 'to secure'. *Procuratemi dell'acqua* would be 'Get me some water'. *Procurarsi* is quite common, meaning 'to get for oneself'. *Mi sono procurato . . .* is 'I have got hold of . . .'.

professionista (m). Professional (*v.* SPORT). An amateur is *un dilettante.*

pronto. 'Ready.' *Lei è sempre pronta ad aiutare* means 'She is always ready to help'. *Pronto soccorso* is 'first aid'. 'Ready, steady, go!' is *Pronti . . . via!* The Spanish word, one of the several taken into English via American from Central America, means 'at once', which is *subito* in Italian. The strange thing, perhaps, is the universal use of *Pronto* on the telephone, meaning 'Hello'. Don't take this any further, however, as I have heard some unknowing people do, and use it as the general word corresponding to 'hello'. It would be ludicrous to call out *pronto* to someone you knew in the street, unless you happened to be telling him that you, or someone else, or something else, were ready.

proposito (m). The special reference here is to the much-used phrase, *a proposito*, which is what you often say if struck by an afterthought, 'Oh, by the way . . . '. *A proposito di . . .* means 'Speaking about . . . ', 'And, on the subject of . . . '. Notice also the expression *fare una cosa di proposito*, which means 'to do something on purpose'. 'On purpose' may also be *con intenzione* (its opposite being *senza intenzione*).

proprio. As an adjective this word corresponds to the French *'propre'*, and Spanish *'propio'* (note the additional *r* in the Italian word), meaning 'own'. *Amor proprio* is *amour propre* or 'self-esteem'. However, it is the use of *proprio* as an adverb that is so common and so important in Italian. The fundamental meanings are 'precisely' and 'really'. *Lui è proprio matto* means 'He is really round the bend'. *Proprio quello che immaginavo!* is 'Just what I thought!' *È proprio una cosa spiacevole* means 'It's something really unpleasant'. *È proprio suo cugino che l'ha fatto* is 'It's (none other than) your cousin who did it'. *Ho ricevuto la lettera proprio stamane* means 'I received the letter this (very) morning'. *Lei giura che è proprio vero* is 'She swears that it is really true'. *Sì, è proprio quello che volevo dire*, 'Yes, that's exactly what I meant'. *No, non conosco proprio nessuno di quelli* means 'No, I don't know a single one of those'. *Penso che per te sarebbe proprio meglio tornare a casa*, 'I think the best thing for you to do would be to go home'. *Non riesco a farlo, non riesco proprio*, 'I can't manage to do it, I really can't'.

prosciutto (m). Ham (*v.* FOOD). *Prosciutto cotto* is 'cooked ham', while *prosciutto crudo* is more 'smoked ham'.

prugna (f). Plum (*v.* FOOD).

pugilato (m). Boxing (*v.* SPORT). 'A boxer' is *un pugile*. 'A boxing-match' is *un incontro*.

pullman (m). Quite sensibly, you'd expect this to mean a pullman railway coach. In fact, it's a comfortably upholstered coach, but not on the railway. So if you hear someone say that he's been somewhere by pullman, he's travelled by road and not rail.

puntina da disegno (f). Drawing pin (*v.* OFFICE).

punto (m). Italians very often use *a un certo punto*. When telling a story they rarely fail to say it. We could translate it literally into English, 'at a certain point', but in Italian it is much more frequent than it is in English. 'Up to a point' would be *fino a un certo punto*. Note that when we say in English, 'The point is that . . .', the Italians say *È il caso che. . . . Punti* (m pl) are just 'points', on which boxers, for instance, win or lose a match. Note also that *punto* is 'full stop', and *punto e virgola* is semi-colon.

puntura (f). Injection, of the kind the doctor gives you. A much-used word for 'puncture' (*v.* CARS) is *bucatura*. Otherwise the correct word is *foratura*.

punzonare. To punch (*v.* OFFICE). *Il punzone* is 'the punch'.

pure. An extremely useful little word to put in in several contexts, to make a sentence sound Italian, which otherwise would be a little stilted. *Andate* means 'Go', while *Andate pure* means 'You may go'. If someone asks your permission to do something you may, of course, answer *Sì* or *Certo*, and so on, but a very common and polite answer is *Fate pure*, which is 'Just do that' and a very Italian way of putting it.

Then, *pure* can have the meaning of *anche*. *Anch'io* means 'So do I' etc, as also does *e io pure*. *Lui vuole andare via e tu pure* means 'He wants to go and so do you'. *È stato trovato pure il suo amico* means 'His friend has been found too'. *Pure allora* gives the idea of 'even then', just as *pure adesso* means 'even now'. Yet another meaning is 'besides', 'what's more', 'moreover'. For example: *Ho ricevuto dieci lettere ieri, e oggi sono arrivati pure due telegrammi*, 'Yesterday I received ten letters, and today two telegrams arrived, moreover'.

Torna pure a casa, che sei stanco e hai bisogno di riposare means 'Just go back home, as you're tired and need rest'.

purtroppo. This exclamation is quite straightforward, meaning 'unfortunately', and is mentioned here in an attempt to persuade people *to use it*, and to dissuade people from over-using what learners do in fact tend to over-use, *sfortunatamente*.

Q

quadro (m). Picture (*v.* HOUSEHOLD).

questione (f). This is the appropriate word to use in 'it's a question of', whereas the question you ask someone is *una domanda*.

Questura (f). Police station, in the large cities. Otherwise we have the term *posto di polizia*.

quindi. One of the most-used words in colloquial Italian. It means 'so', 'therefore', 'consequently'. *Fa caldo oggi, quindi vado alla spiaggia* means 'It's hot today, so I'm going to the beach'. *Mi ha detto che non poteva venire, quindi non so che cosa fare*, 'He told me that he couldn't come, and so I don't know what to do'. *Ha cominciato a strillare, e quindi è stato messo fuori*, 'He started to shout, and so he was put outside'. You will quite often hear the word used by itself, as a complete idea, as, indeed, many people use the English 'So'. Someone may explain something, and the implications are clear, and you say just *Quindi*, meaning that you realize what the consequences are, or you appreciate his state of mind, or something else. Again, in interviews, *Quindi* is a common word. The person being interviewed has just answered one question, and this leads the questioner on to another question, which he will begin with *Quindi* . . . . For example, *Quindi è contento, sul serio?* 'So you're really happy?'

R

racchia (f). An ugly girl or woman, a 'horror'.

raccogliere. 'To collect', 'to gather', 'to put together'. *Raccogliere francobolli* is 'to collect stamps'. *Raccogliere le forze* is 'to gather one's strength'. *Raccogliere* is also the usual verb for 'to pick up'. In an office, *un raccoglitore* is a hard-backed file-cover, a cover in which you can file papers.

raccomandare. 'To recommend.' Note the double *c* and single *m* of the Italian word, as against the single *c* and the double *m* of the English one. And speaking of letters (the sort you post), this verb means 'to register'.

The important point to note, however, is that the reflexive form, *raccomandarsi*, is used when you wish to stress a point to someone. *Vi raccomando* is approximately 'Pay special attention to', 'Don't forget', 'Be sure to do it', and so on. *Mi raccomando, non chiudere mai quella porta* means 'Be sure never to close that door'. It's very usual to add this word at the end of a telephone conversation, in which an order has been given, to make sure that the order really will be carried out. To render the English 'recommend' it is best to take the verb *consigliare*.

radazza (f). Mop, squeegee (*v.* HOUSEHOLD).

radiatore (m). Radiator (*v.* CARS).

radice (f). Radish (*v.* FOOD). *Radice* is also the word for 'root', 'origin', and so on.

raffreddore (m). The common cold, so don't go catching a *freddo*. *Temo che stia per venirmi un bel raffreddore* means 'I'm afraid I'm in for a heavy cold'.

ragione (f). You will so often hear *Ha ragione*, 'You're right', or *Lui non ha ragione*, 'He's wrong', and suchlike, that it's worth a mention. If you are in agreement with something that someone is saying, you can slip in *e con ragione* at the right time to show this—'and quite right, too'. *Per quale ragione?* is, of course, 'Why, for what reason?' Another frequent combination is *per qualsiasi ragione*, 'for any reason whatever'. *Dare ragione* is also used in this way: *I resultati mi hanno dato ragione*, meaning 'I have been proved right by the results'.

ragioniere (m). Accountant (*v.* OFFICE). Also 'book-keeper'. That which is done, 'accountancy' or 'book-keeping', is called *ragioneria*.

rana (f). Frog. In swimming, the 'breast stroke' (*v.* SPORT).

rapa (f). Turnip (*v.* FOOD).

rasoio (m). Razor 'A safety-razor' is *un rasoio di sicurezza*. 'An electric razor' is *un rasoio elettrico* (*v.* HOUSEHOLD). 'To shave' is either *radersi* or, more commonly, *farsi la barba*.

razza (f). This word, meaning 'race', 'breed' etc., is extremely common in the exclamation *Che razza di . . . !* 'What a . . . !' It is also important to realize that this word corresponds more or less to the English 'sort', as in *Che razza di lavoro!* Note the pejorative indication.

recarsi. 'To go to a place'. *Ieri mi sono recato alla palestra . . .* means 'Yesterday I went to the gymnasium . . .'.

reggersi. 'To hold on to' something. *Reggersi in piedi* is 'to stay on one's feet', 'to be able to remain standing'. *Alla fine della quinta ripresa il pugile non ha potuto reggersi in piedi*, 'At the end of the fifth round the boxer was not able to stay on his feet'. *Non si regge* means 'It won't hold' or 'It won't hold up'.

registratore (m). Tape-recorder. It may also be 'registrar'.

rendersi. Literally 'to render to oneself'. There are various ways of translating the word according to the context, but I include it here solely to point out the meaning of *rendersi conto*, which is 'to realize'. Remember that the past participle is *reso. Mi sono reso conto che . . .* means 'I realized that . . .'.

resto (m). Two things here. Firstly, it means 'change' such as you hope to get back from 5,000 lire when the bill is 4,500 lire, and secondly, in the expression *del resto* it is much used, this meaning 'anyway', 'at any rate', 'besides', 'after all'. *Non capisci proprio niente—del resto sei troppo giovane*, 'You don't understand anything at all—after all, you're too young'.

ribes (m). Currant (v. FOOD).

riga (f). 'Line', the sort you draw with a ruler. A 'ruler' can be *rigatrice* (f), and may also be a *metro* (m), or *riga*.

rimanere. One meaning of this verb is quite straightforward, 'to remain'. *Rimanere a casa* means 'to stay at home'. However, the verb is used in a good many ways where we could not use 'to remain', 'to stay', 'to be left' or anything similar in English. In several expressions *rimanere* gives the idea of 'to become', although I do not mean to say that it would be possible to use the English word in rendering the meaning. For instance, *Cinque persone sono rimaste uccise ieri in un tragico scontro*, 'Five people were killed yesterday in a tragic accident'. But, *Fortunatamente, è rimasto illeso*, which is 'Luckily he was uninjured'. In this case it would be possible to use 'to remain'. One of the commonest expressions using *rimanere* is *rimanere molto male*, 'to be very disappointed'. *Sono rimasto molto male* is 'I was very disappointed'. Also one may say *rimane sorpreso, rimane sbalordito* and *rimane di sasso*, that is 'he's surprised', 'he's flabbergasted', or 'amazed', and 'he's petrified', or 'he's dumbfounded'. *Rimanere in forse* is 'to be kept waiting for the result', 'to be left in suspense'. You may also hear people asking the way by using this word—*Dove rimane . . . ?* In reporting that certain people were in agreement on some point, Italians may well state that *Loro sono rimasti d'accordo circa* or *su . . .*—that is, 'They were in agreement about . . .'.

In short, *rimanere* is a verb you will do well to cultivate, and especially bearing in mind that as like as not the meaning will deviate from the seeming one of 'to remain'.

rinfresco (m). Refreshment (v. FOOD).

riparazione (f). Repair (v. CARS).

ripieno. 'Filled' (v. FOOD).

ripresa (f). 'Round' (v. SPORT). This refers to boxing, while in games with divisions other than rounds, *ripresa* may be 'half', for example. On the subject of boxing, you will also often hear and read the English word 'round' (perhaps without the u, *'rond'*), this demonstrating the English influence on the vocabulary of the sport. There are many instances of the English word being used, although you would at times find it difficult to recognize it. 'Clinch', 'uppercut', 'ring' are some examples.

riscaldare. 'To heat'. *Riscaldamento centrale* (m) is 'central heating'. In Italy this is quite common. For heating water, you frequently find a *scaldabagno* (m), an 'electric water heater' or 'geyser'. In a car, the heating unit is called *riscaldatore* (m) (*v.* CARS).

riserva (f). Reserve (*v.* SPORT).

riso (m). Rice (*v.* FOOD).

rispondere. I put this in to remind you that it is the word for 'to reply', 'to answer'. The answer itself is *la risposta*. At the same time, remember that 'to ask a question' is *domandare* or *chiedere*.

ristorante (m). Restaurant (*v.* SHOPS). *See also* **trattoria, rosticceria** and **tavola calda.**

risultare. *Dalla conversazione risulta che la ragazza potrebbe continuare a lavorare qui solo se chiedesse permesso speciale,* 'From the conversation it appears (*or* turns out) that the girl could continue working here only if she requested special permission'. It would be stretching the point somewhat to say 'result' in this context in English. As with *rimanere* (*q.v.*), for example, almost the exact word exists in English, and is used, but for just one of the meanings of the Italian verb, while in fact other meanings are more common.

To put this diagrammatically:

to turn out, to prove to be	*risultare*
to result	*risultare*
to follow, to ensue	*risultare* or *seguire*
to appear	*risultare* or *sembrare*

One's first reaction is usually to imagine that such a verb must be of very limited usage, while this is not in fact so. *Risultare* is used a lot in everyday Italian. The most satisfactory translations are usually 'to turn out to be', 'to prove to be' and 'to appear'. *Risulta che non vuole continuare* is 'It turns out that he/she doesn't want to continue'. 'The result' is *il risultato*.

ritardo (m). 'Delay.' The word is included here because of the common expression *arrivare con . . . di ritardo*, which is 'to arrive . . . late'. *Giovanni è arrivato con due ore di ritardo* means 'John arrived two hours late'.

riunione (f). A 'meeting', not necessarily a 'reunion'.

rivedere. 'To see again'. You must be conversant with the Italian 'goodbye', *arrivederci*, or alternatively *arrivederla*.

rivista (f). 'A magazine', of the sort you buy on bookstalls. The Italian *magazzino* is a 'store, large shop'. *Rivista* also corresponds to the English 'review'.

roba (f). 'Stuff', 'things'. You can just imagine how much such a word can be used. *Cosa è questa roba?* means 'What's this stuff here?' *C'è qualche roba da mangiare?* is 'Is there anything to eat?' *Non mi piace questa roba* means 'I don't like this stuff'. *Ho visto un mucchio di roba sulla sua scrivania* means 'I saw a whole heap of stuff on his desk'. If you have already studied Spanish, you will be conversant with the word *ropa*, meaning strictly 'clothes', but the Italian word is, as you can see, of very much wider application. And apart from being applied to material things, it can be used to mean 'A fine thing, too!' referring to the situation. *Bella roba!*

rognoni (m pl). Kidneys (*v.* FOOD).

romanesco (m). This is the dialect of Rome, sometimes called *romano* and at times, pejoratively, *romanaccio*. Now a dialect is not just a different accent, comprising as it does not only this different pronunciation, but also changed grammatical forms and in particular a special vocabulary of its own. *Romanesco* refers more to this passed-on old dialect, while people are thinking more of the slangy words in the dialect when they refer to it as *romanaccio*. This is not to be a treatise on the Roman dialect, but it is worth while mentioning a few general points about it. The pronunciation tends to be more voiced than ordinary Italian, and endings of words are cut off, often missing the last syllable altogether. This is especially noticeable in the case of infinitives, *capire* becoming *capì*, for example, and *andare* becoming *annà*. In this last example there is an indication of another point, the substitution of the combination *nd* by *nn*. Where Italian has the combination *gl*, as in *moglie*, Romanesco has a written *j*, pronounced as an *i*. *Moglie* therefore becomes *moje*. Then you have other occasional letter changes. *Il* is *er*, *del* is *der* and so on, although note that there is no universal substitution of *l* for *r*. The indefinite article loses its vowel, becoming just *n*. 'A friend of mine' for instance, is *'n amico mio*.

I have no intention of including any vocabulary list here; suffice it to point out that the vocabulary is pure Italian, with a number of vogue words and a few, just a few, real dialect words: for example, *Ella è ita* instead of *è andata*. Before making one or two short quotations in Romanesco, I must point out that they often double what are really single consonants (or drop one of what are really double ones!). For example, *subbito* instead of *subito*. Now here are a few quotations:

Roma, infatti, s'è spopolata. Tanti se ne so' iti in montagna, tant'artri ar mare. Pochi so' rimasti. Pe' me, tutti ponno partì; io nun farò artro che accompagnalli a' la stazione, ripetenno a me stesso: Io, da bôn Romano, lontano da Fontan de' Trevi e da Trinità de' Monti nun ce saprebbe vive manco un giorno.

You will immediately see the deviations from Italian—*sono* becomes *so'*, *altri* is *artri*, *possono* becomes *ponno*, *partire* is *partì*, *accompagnarli* is *accompagnalli*, *non* becomes *nun*, *buon* is *bôn*, and so on.

One more quotation:

Nun pò annà avanti così. Io nun vojo fà der male a nisuno, ma pretenno un tantinello de comprensione. Io so' quer poro disgrazziato che abbita lassù, all'attico. Mò, cor fatto che voi ciavete sto cinema all'operto. . . . Perhaps you need to be told that *quer poro* is *quel povero*, but otherwise you should be able to make it out. Note the word *mò*, here, as often, meaning something like 'well'. In Rome, you will hear this *mò* so very many times.

You will no doubt have understood that the above extract is the beginning of a Roman's complaint to the manager of a cinema about the noise coming up to his apartment above the cinema. During the summer all possible openings in the cinema are taken advantage of, and if you live near one you are liable to be disturbed by the noise.

rombo (m). Turbot (*v.* FOOD).

rondella (f). Washer (*v.* HOUSEHOLD). This refers to the 'tap washer', and not to the 'washing machine', which is *una lavatrice*.

rossoneri (m pl). Milan F.C. (*v.* SPORT). Another example of football teams being referred to by their colours.

rosticceria (f). Shop where you can buy roast meats. We could call it a 'roast meat shop', or even a 'restaurant', as you can eat the roast food there, in most cases.

rubare. To rob or to steal. Note also the words *rapire* (to rape, to kidnap), *rapinare* (to rob), *rapinatore* (m) (robber), and *rapitore* (m) (abductor, kidnapper). *Un furto* refers to theft or robbery.

rubinetto (m). 'Tap' (*v.* HOUSEHOLD). *Rubinetto del gas* is 'gas tap'.

S

salamoia (f). Pickles (*v.* FOOD).

sale (m). Salt (*v.* FOOD). The shop marked '*Sali & Tabacchi*' sells, of course, salt and tobacco, and you will probably find the combination rather mystifying. Actually, both salt and tobacco are commodities of which there is a state monopoly, and this accounts for their having to be bought in a special shop—although the shop also sells other things, such as note-paper, toothpaste and so on.

salire. A bit of a false friend for those who know Spanish. The Italian verb means 'to go up', 'to rise'. *Salire le scale* is 'to go up the stairs'. *Salire in autobus* is 'to board a bus'. 'To go out' (the meaning of the Spanish verb) is *uscire* in Italian.

salmone (m). Salmon (*v.* FOOD).

salsa (f). 'Sauce', 'gravy' (*v.* FOOD). *Salsa di pomodoro* is 'tomato sauce', 'tomato ketchup'.

salsamenteria (f). 'Grocer's shop' (*v.* SHOPS). From country to country you obviously find some shops existing in some countries which do not exist in others, and other shops offering different selections of goods to such an extent that it is difficult to find a good equivalent in another language. In Italian, for example, there is the *drogheria*, which sells not drugs, but herbs, soap-powder, brooms, cotton-wool, toothpaste, dried fruit, razor blades and various other articles. I prefer to call it a 'general store'. *Salsamenteria* is certainly the nearest to the English 'grocer's', with perhaps more accent on delica-tessen. You cannot, however, purchase salt here, as it comes under state monopoly, and must be bought in a shop (*see* **sale**) specially licensed for the purpose.

salsiccia (f). Sausage (*v.* FOOD).

saltare. 'To jump.' 'A jump' is *un salto*. In sport, the various jumps are: *salto in alto* (high jump), *salto in lungo* (long jump), *salto con l'asta* (pole vault) and *salto triplo* (hop, step and jump).

salutare. Too elementary to be a false friend, no doubt. It can of course be 'to salute', militarily. In common use, however, it is 'to greet (to say hello)' and 'to bid farewell'. *Saluta la signora*, says the mother to the little boy on taking leave of Mrs. Smith, 'Say goodbye to Mrs. Smith'. Perhaps one might say *Ti saluto* on leaving someone, whereas we should hardly say 'I salute you' in English.

salute (f). Not 'a salute' (which is *un saluto*), but 'health'. The point to notice is the use of the word when having a drink. *Salute* corresponds to 'Cheers'.

salvia (f). 'Sage' (*v.* FOOD).

sangue (m). 'Blood'. As in French, this word is masculine, whereas it is feminine in Spanish. *Sangue freddo*, you will say must be 'cold blood'. And it is. You can kill people in cold blood also in Italy—although it is more likely to be a *'crime de passion'*. However, Italians commonly use *sangue freddo* to mean 'keep calm'. Mike Bongiorno, a favourite TV personality for years, always advises competitors in his quiz programmes to keep *calma e sangue freddo*, when a critical position has been reached, 'Keep cool, calm and collected, now!'

sardina (f). 'Sardine' (*v*. FOOD).

sartoria (f). The place where the *sarto* or *sarta* works, namely the 'tailor's' (*v*. SHOPS).

sbarra spaziatrice (f). Space bar, on the typewriter (*v*. OFFICE).

sbornia (f). 'Drunken feeling', 'intoxication'. *Prendere la sbornia* is 'to get tight'.

sbrigarsi. 'To hurry, hasten, make haste, buck up'. *Sbrigati* means 'Come on, hurry up, buck your ideas up'. *Me la sbrigherò* means 'I'll hurry it along', 'I'll buck it up'. *Una briga* is 'a care', 'some trouble'. *Dare briga a qualcuno* is 'to give someone a lot of trouble'. *Darsi la briga* is 'to take on something difficult, to make exertions'.

scaffale (m). 'Shelf.' *Scaffale da archivio* is 'filing cupboard' (*v*. OFFICE).

scala (f). Stairs, staircase, ladder (*v*. HOUSEHOLD). 'A stepladder' is *una scala a gradini piani, una scala trasportabile*. In music or geography, *scala* is 'scale'. 'A spiral staircase' is *una scala a chiocciola*.

scaldabagno (m). 'Geyser', 'water heater' (*v*. HOUSEHOLD).

scalpello (m). Not a 'scalpel', which is *bisturi a un solo taglio*, but a 'chisel'.

scappamento (m). Exhaust. The 'exhaust pipe' is the *tubo di scappamento* (m) (*v*. CARS).

scarica (f). 'Discharge', electrical or of a gun. The plural *scariche* refers to 'atmospherics'. The verb is *scaricare*, meaning 'to unload', 'to discharge'.

scarico d'acqua (m). Water drain (*v*. HOUSEHOLD). *Scarico di troppo pieno* is 'overflow pipe'.

scatola (f). 'Box.' It may also be a 'tin'. The 'gearbox' is called *scatola del cambio* or *scatola degli ingranaggi* (*v*. CARS). *Mettere in scatola* is the verb 'to can', and *in scatola* means 'canned', 'tinned'.

scattare. 'To sprint.' *Far scattare una molla*, for instance, is 'to release a spring'. 'Sprinter' is *scattatore* (m) (*v*. SPORT).

scemo (m). This word means 'lunatic', 'someone touched', an 'idiot'. 'He's not quite all there', 'He's a bit touched' or 'He's a bit crazy' would be *È mezzo scemo*.

scheda (f). 'Card' (but not of the 'postcard' variety, which is *cartolina postale*). *Schedare* is the verb, meaning 'to card-index'. 'The card-index' itself is called *schedario* (*v.* OFFICE).

scherma (f). 'Fencing' (*v.* SPORT).

scherzo (m). Joke. The verb is *scherzare*, and you can also *fare scherzi*. The verb corresponds largely to our 'to kid', and some people use it very frequently. *Che scherzi* or *Scherzi*, 'Are you kidding?' 'It's no joke', and so on.

schienale (m). 'Back of seat' (*v.* CARS).

schifo (m). 'It makes me sick' (figuratively) is usually *mi fa schifo*. This word is to be avoided in the best Italian, but it is of very common usage in everyday speaking. *Una cosa schifosa* is 'something that makes you sick'. *Che schifo!* is an exclamation which indicates 'How horrible!' In some places, Naples for instance, the word has not such a strong meaning, owing to the fact that it is in more frequent use there than elsewhere.

sciacquare. 'To rinse'. Many times have I heard housewives at a loss as to how to tell their maids to rinse the clothes. 'To hang out the washing' is *stendere la roba*.

sciocco. A false friend. It means 'silly', whereas 'a shock' is usually *una scossa*. So do not think this refers to something shocking. Remember that it means 'silly', 'stupid', 'foolish' etc. *È sciocco da parte mia* means 'It's stupid of me'. The corresponding noun is *sciocchezza* (f), which means 'something foolish', 'nonsense' and so on. 'An electric shock' is *una scossa elettrica*. Something that shocks you can be *offensivo*, *rivoltante*, *orribile* and so forth. *La ragazza provò una forte emozione* would be 'The girl got a proper shock'.

scioperare. 'To strike', in the sense of not going to work. The strike itself is *lo sciopero*, while a 'striker' is a *scioperante*. 'To be on strike' may be *essere in isciopero*, or else *scioperare*. A 'blackleg' is *un crumiro*.

scirocco (m). The sirocco wind, which is hot and humid and blows from the south, making Rome, for example, no place for a tourist when it is blowing. The temperature may be in the nineties, but no matter, if there is no *scirocco* to make it sweaty and very heavy going.

scivolare. 'To slip', 'to slide', perhaps 'to skid', although this is more exactly *slittare* (*v.* CARS).

scocciare. The dictionary tells you that this means 'to unhook', 'to shell eggs' and so on, but this is of little consequence. The important thing is that *scocciare* is another of the verbs meaning 'to bore'. *È troppo scocciante!* means 'It's too boring!' *See also* **seccante**.

scolo (m). Drain (*v.* HOUSEHOLD).

scombro (m). Mackerel (*v.* FOOD).

sconosciuto. 'Unknown.' I include this as people do tend to forget, or rather not to call to mind at the requisite moment, these words beginning with *s* and meaning the opposite of the word without the *s*. *Scomposto*, for example, means 'ruffled, disconcerted', while *composto* is 'unruffled, composed'.

sconto (m). This means 'discount', and is perfectly straightforward, the reason for mentioning it here being that it is of such widespread use in Italy. Some people make a point of asking for *uno sconto* whatever they buy and wherever they buy it. 'Couldn't you possibly make a little reduction for me?' The practice of haggling over prices is regional, strong in the south and taboo in much of the north of the country. In the parts where they indulge in the *sconto* system, they more or less expect you to ask for a *sconto* when you buy something. The verb is *scontare*. The verb 'to bargain', 'to haggle', is *trattare*. The *tasso ufficiale di sconto* is the 'bank rate'.

scontro (m). 'Crash', 'collision' (*v.* CARS).

scopa (f). 'Broom' (*v.* HOUSEHOLD). *Scopare* is 'to sweep'.

scopo (m). One of several words meaning 'aim', 'intention', 'purpose', 'object' and so on. *Allo scopo di fare una cosa* is 'with the object of doing something'. *Con che scopo?* asks 'For what purpose?' I stress this word, as learners usually pass it over, probably thinking that it means 'scope', which it doesn't.

scoprire. This is an easy verb, but remember its double meaning: 'to discover' (*fare una scoperta*) and 'to uncover'.

scordarsi. An alternative to *dimenticare*, 'to forget'.

scorta (f). 'Store' or 'stock', or else 'spare'. *Una ruota di scorta* is 'a spare wheel'. *Scorta* may also be 'escort' or 'convoy', and the corresponding verb, 'to escort' or 'to convoy', is *scortare*.

scrivania (f). 'Desk' (*v.* OFFICE). 'The cash desk', on the other hand, is *la cassa*.

scrivere. Note that 'to type' is *scrivere a macchina*, while the 'typewriter' is *macchina da scrivere*. Another way to say 'to type' is *battere a macchina*, and this is in fact the usual term. A 'writer' is *scrittore*, and 'handwriting' is *scrittura* (f). A 'writing desk' may be either *scrittoio* or *scrivania*.

scuola guida (f). 'Driving school' (*v.* CARS).

scusarsi. This is the usual verb for 'to apologize', and also to say 'Excuse me'. Remember that if you wish to pass someone, or wish someone to get out of your way, you say *Permesso*. *Mi scusi* is definitely to make an excuse for having done something. *Scusi . . .* is a very common way to begin asking someone you don't know to tell you something. Having inconvenienced someone, you often say on leaving *Mi scusi tanto* (or you could content yourself with *Mi dispiace*).

sdrucciolevole. 'Slippery' (*v.* CARS). *Una strada sdrucciolevole* is 'a slippery road'.

seccante. This is the same as *noioso*, 'boring'. *È molto seccante, purtroppo* means 'He is unfortunately very boring'. The verb *seccare* means 'to bore' and, in its reflexive form, *seccarsi*, 'to be bored'. *Che seccatura!* means 'How boring!' or 'What a bore!' *See also* **scocciare**.

secchio (m). 'Bucket' (*v.* HOUSEHOLD).

secco. Speaking of money, or rather lack of it, *essere a secco* is 'to be very hard up', perhaps 'to be stony broke' (or you may say *essere al verde*).

secondo. As a noun, it may be 'second', as one-sixtieth of a minute, or as an assistant in a duel or in boxing (*v.* SPORT). It also means 'second', meaning 'next after first', of course. But the important thing to note here is its use meaning 'according to'. *Secondo mio fratello* means 'according to my brother'. *Secondo il vostro desiderio* is 'in accordance with your wish'. Note, too, that it may be used as an alternative to *dipende*, meaning 'it depends'. For example: *Mi aiuterà?— Secondo.* ('Will you help me?' 'It depends'.)

sedano (m). 'Celery' (*v.* FOOD).

sede (f). 'Head office', 'central office', 'seat' (of government, etc.) (*v.* OFFICE). *La Santa Sede* is 'The Holy See'.

sedia (f). 'Chair' (*v.* HOUSEHOLD).

sedile (m). 'Seat' (*v.* CARS). *Un sedile anteriore* is 'a front seat', and 'back seat' is *sedile posteriore*. The arm-rest at the side is *il bracciolo*, and the back of the seat is the *schienale* (m).

sega (f). 'Saw' (*v.* HOUSEHOLD). The verb is *segare*.

segmento (m). 'Piston ring' (*v.* CARS).

segretario (m). 'Male secretary'. *Segretaria* is the word for the more usual female secretary. The office where secretaries work is *la segreteria*. To obtain information, for example, you are sometimes requested to present yourself *in segreteria*.

semiasse (m). 'Axle-shaft' (*v.* CARS).

senape (f). 'Mustard' (*v.* FOOD).

sensato. This is the usual adjective for our 'sensible', meaning 'not silly', 'prudent', 'intelligent'. Do not say *sensibile* (*q.v.*), which is usually 'sensitive'.

sensibile. A famous false friend, meaning 'sensitive'. *Sono molto sensibile ai cattivi odori* means 'I'm very sensitive to bad smells'. *Sensibilmente* usually refers to another meaning of *sensibile*, namely 'noticeable' (*i.e.* 'that can be measured'). *Ha diminuito sensibilmente* means 'It has decreased noticeably'. *See also* **sensato** *above*.

sentenza (f). 'Judgment' (and 'sentence' in this sense). A sentence in the grammatical sense is *una frase* or *proposizione* (f).

sentire. I am well aware that there is a long list of possible meanings in the dictionary, but in almost every case there is another verb possible, and it is nearly always this other verb which is used. For example, the dictionary says that *sentire* means 'to touch', but we mostly use the other verb given, *toccare*. There is no question that, to most people, *sentire* is the accepted way of saying *udire*, 'to hear'. Of course, if you use it reflexively, you automatically think of how you are feeling. *Mi sento male*, for example. But, I repeat, 'to hear' is the meaning which springs to mind. You will so often hear *Senti* and *Senta*. Many housewives say, or rather shout, this word as they enter a shop, in order to attract attention and to try to avoid waiting their turn. You could say it was the same as the English 'I say!' but used much more frequently. If you go up to someone to ask something, you should begin, politely, *Per cortesia . . .* or *Scusi . . .* , but very often people do say *Senta . . . .*

senza. This means 'without', as you must know. *Senza fallo* is 'without fail', and *senza dubbio* is 'without doubt'. These are common enough dictionary expressions. *Senza complimenti*, on the other hand, you will look hard to find under *senza*, yet you will hear it used very often. You may offer someone a cigarette, for example, and seeing him hesitant about taking one, you may say *Prego, senza complimenti*, meaning 'Go on, please take one', that is to say, 'it's a genuine offer'. Perhaps you have handed your guest the plate of biscuits, and she has declined, whereupon you have another go. She may very likely then say *senza complimenti*, meaning that she really doesn't want one. Accompanying a friend to visit another of his friends, you may well be invited to come in and sit down *senza complimenti*, 'Do come in and sit down' ('We're not formal, come in and feel at home'). *Non faccia complimenti*, by the way, means 'Don't do/say it for formality's sake' *i.e.* 'Say what you really think'.

 Senz'altro is one of the common ways of saying 'of course', 'surely'. *Non posso venire domani, ma vengo senz'altro dopodomani* means 'I can't come tomorrow, but I'll come the next day for sure'. *Posso usare il telefono?—Senz'altro.* ('May I use the telephone?' 'Of course'.)

 Senza ingranaggi is 'gearless' (*v.* CARS).

seppia (f). 'Squid' (*v.* FOOD).

serbatoio (m). 'Tank' or 'reservoir'. *Serbatoio benzina* is 'petrol tank', and *serbatoio del liquido dei freni* is 'brake fluid supply tank' (*v.* CARS).

serie (f). 'Series' or 'set'. *In grande serie* is 'mass production'. *Un modello fuori serie* is 'a custom-built model'. In football, *Serie A* corresponds to the English First Division and *Serie B* to the Second Division (*v.* SPORT).

serratura (f). 'Lock'. *Il buco della serratura* is 'the keyhole'.

servizi (m pl). Speaking of the gas, electricity, water and other services of a town, these are the 'public utilities'. 'Social Services' are *servizi sociali*. Advertisements for houses tell you what floor it is on (the *attico* or 'penthouse' being at a premium), how many rooms there are, and how many *servizi* there are (*doppii, tripli* and so on). This refers to the bathrooms and like rooms. Commonly a flat will have 'double services', the main bathroom and another one where there is a tub to do the washing, or a smaller room with washbasin and W.C.

servizio da tè (m). 'Tea service' (*v.* HOUSEHOLD).

seta (f). 'Silk' (*v.* HOUSEHOLD).

sfrontato. 'Cheeky', 'impudent', 'saucy', 'brazen'.

sfruttare. 'To take advantage of', 'to exploit'.

sfumatura (f). Nuance. *È difficile capire tutte le sfumature in questo libro*, 'It's hard to understand all the shades of meaning in this book'.

sgabuzzino (m). 'Closet', 'cupboard', the little room where the cleaning implements are stored.

sguardo (m). *Uno sguardo* is 'a glance'. It may also be 'a peephole'.

sidro (m). 'Cider' (*v.* FOOD).

siepe (f). 'Hedge' or 'fence'. In athletics, *siepi* refers to the 'steeplechase' (*v.* SPORT).

signore (m or f pl). Remember, and avoid, the easily understandable error of those who know no Italian, or very little, that *signore* can be either the masculine singular, meaning 'sir' (not the title, of course), or the feminine plural, meaning 'ladies'. Confusion often leads to embarrassment, and in fact many public conveniences use *uomini* and *donne*.

silenziatore (m). 'Silencer' (*v.* CARS).

simpatico. This adjective means 'pleasant', as you are probably already aware, or 'nice' or some such thing, but not 'sympathetic', which is *compassionevole* or *comprensivo*.
Simpatico is used very much indeed, of people in particular but also of things. The opposite is also common, *antipatico*, 'unpleasant', 'nasty'. A *simpaticone* is a 'very likeable person'.

sindaco (m). Quite simply, and surprisingly, this is the 'mayor'. His term of office is his *sindacato*, which also means what you would expect it to mean, 'syndicate'.

sistemare. A verb you very often come across. The basic meaning is 'to arrange', 'to fix'. *Senz'altro potremo sistemare qualcosa per loro* means 'Certainly we'll be able to fix something up for them'. *Può sistemare il rubinetto, per piacere?* means 'Can you fix the tap, please?' *Non so come si può sistemare la faccenda* is 'I don't know how we can arrange this business'. *Ho chiesto al capo se esisteva la possibilità di sistemare le cose* means 'I've asked the boss if there was any chance of arranging things'. *Proviamo la nuova macchina. Ci sistemiamo tutti e quattro e via.* 'Let's try out the new car. All four of us get in, and away we go.'

The noun is *sistema*, and this, you will remember, is masculine—*un sistema*. *Sistema di ingranaggi* is the 'gearing' (*v.* CARS).

slittare. 'To skid' (*v.* CARS). 'A skid' is *una slittata*.

smettere. 'To leave off', 'to stop'. *Smettere il lavoro* is 'to knock off work'. *Ha smesso di piovere* means 'It's stopped raining'. *Smettila!* means 'That's enough!' 'Stop it!' 'Put a sock in it!' and so on.

sogliola (f). 'Sole', as in 'Dover sole' (*v.* FOOD). The sole of the foot is *la pianta del piede*, while the sole of a shoe is *la suola di una scarpa*.

sogni d'oro (m pl). 'Sweet dreams' or 'sleep tight'. From the noun *sogno*, meaning 'dream'.

soldi (m pl). 'Money'. This is far and away the most-used Italian word for money. Remember that it is used in the plural. *Denaro* is also possible, of course, but *soldi* is the universal word. If you are unlucky enough to be completely broke, then you are *senza un soldo*, 'without a bean'. Otherwise you could use *essere a secco* (*see* **secco**).

solito. *Al solito* is 'as usual'. Remember the accent on the first syllable. *Alla solita ora* means 'at the usual time'. *Come al solito* is 'just as usual'.

sono io. 'Who is it?' What do you answer to this question? 'It's I'?—'It's me'?—'I'?—'Me'? In Italian, at any rate, you say *Sono io*, literally 'I am I'. On the phone, if you hear someone asking for you, you say *Sono io*, 'Speaking'. Notice the same construction, too, when in English we say 'It is I (me) who said that', *Sono stato io che l'ho detto*. You cannot begin *È io* . . . .

spago (m). 'String.'

spazzola (f). 'Brush' (*v.* HOUSEHOLD). *Spazzolare* is 'to brush'. 'A clothes brush' is *una spazzola da abiti*, *spazzola da capelli* is 'hair-brush', and *spazzola da scarpe* is 'shoe-brush'. The diminutive form, *spazzolino* (m), is used for a 'tooth-brush', for example, which is *spazzolino per i denti*.

specchio (m). 'Mirror.' The 'rear-view mirror' on a car is *specchio retrovisivo* (v. CARS).

spedire. 'To send', 'to dispatch'. 'The dispatch department' is *la spedizione* (v. OFFICE). Note that 'to post a letter' is *imbucare una lettera*.

spegnere. 'To put out', 'to switch off'. *Spegnere la luce* is 'to turn the light off', and *spegnere il motore* is 'to switch off the engine' (v. CARS). The opposite is *accendere*.

spensierato. 'Carefree.'

spettacolo (m). This is the usual word for 'show', 'performance'. *Il più grande spettacolo del mondo* is 'the greatest show on earth'. *È uno spettacolo magnifico* is 'It's a wonderful show'.

spicci (m pl). 'Change', of the sort the conductor always asks you for. The dictionary gives you the word *spicciolo*, but in practice you will find the plural form, *spicci* or *spiccioli*, always used. Occasionally you hear the singular *spiccio*, but not the older, long form. *Cinque lire spicce*, says the bus conductor hopefully, as everybody hands him either a fifty-lire coin or a one-hundred lire one.

spillo (m). 'Pin' (v. HOUSEHOLD). 'Safety pin' is *spillo da balia* or *spillo di sicurezza*.

spina (f). 'Plug', of the sort that is plugged into a socket. *Una spina tripolare*, for example, is 'a three-pin plug'. 'The socket' is *la presa* (v. HOUSEHOLD).

spinaci (m pl). 'Spinach' (v. FOOD).

spingere. 'To push', 'to shove', 'to thrust'. The noun is *una spinta*, and *dare una spinta a qualcuno* is 'to give someone a push'. You will see *spingere* on doors which you are expected to push to open.

spinoso. Literally 'thorny', 'spiny'. Referring to a problem, if it is *spinoso* it is a tricky one.

spiritoso. 'Clever' or 'witty'. *Non fare lo spiritoso* is 'Aren't you clever?' and so on.

spogliatoio (m). This is the dressing-room, or rather the 'undressing-room'. At the seaside, in a *stabilimento* (q.v.), if you are not fortunate enough to get a cabin, or prefer not to have one, you may pay to use the *spogliatoio*, the 'changing-room'.

spogliatrice (f). This derives from the verb *spogliarsi*, 'to undress'. Indeed, the performer of this action does just that, undresses herself, and in public, and in a provocative manner, for she is a 'strip-tease dancer'.

spolverare. 'To dust'. A 'duster' is normally called a *straccio*, which is a pretty general word for any sort of cleaning rag.

sport (m). *Lo sport* is the general word for, naturally, 'sport'. *Sport invernale* is 'winter sports' (*v.* SPORT).

sportello (m). 'Booking office', 'ticket window' and so on (*v.* OFFICE). Door of a car.

spremuta (f). 'Squash', of the sort you drink.

spruzzatore (m). 'Jet' (*v.* CARS).

spumante (m). This refers to *vino spumante*, 'sparkling wine', wine of the champagne variety.

spuntino (m). 'Snack' (*v.* FOOD).

sputare. 'To spit.' *Sputare fuori soldi* is 'fork out money'. *Sputare sangue* is 'to spit blood'.

squadra (f). 'Team.' *La squadra ospite* is 'the home team' (*v.* SPORT).

squillo (m). 'Ring', 'ringing sound'. The newspapers are occasionally full of the latest scandal about the *ragazze squillo*, 'call girls'.

stabilimento (m). 'Factory' or 'establishment', perhaps, but the special meaning of this word is in connexion with the seaside. In many resorts the whole stretch of sand is divided up among private *stabilimenti* or 'beach-stations'. This means that to have a swim, or even to get within hailing distance of the sea, you have to pay to enter the beach-station, where you will (usually) get a cabin in which to leave and lock up your clothes etc. Some *stabilimenti* are quite luxurious, others less so. They have to provide certain amenities, and there are beach guards and police on duty, if not always in evidence. There are changing-rooms (*spogliatoii*) (*q.v.*), bars, restaurant, showers and so on. If you don't care to pay for your swim, you'll have to find a *spiaggia libera*, 'free beach', but in some places this is a hard task.

stabilire. 'To establish', 'to fix', 'to ascertain', 'to find out'. *Primo devo stabilire il suo livello della lingua* means 'First I have to find out his standard of knowledge of the language'. *Stabilire un nuovo primato mondiale* is 'to set up a new world record'. The one who holds the record, the 'record-holder', is called the *primatista*.

staffetta (f). The baton used in relay races, and so the name given to the race itself. The 4×400 *staffetta* is the 400 metres relay (*v.* SPORT).

stagione (f). 'Season' (*v.* SPORT).

stantuffo (m). 'Piston' (*v.* CARS).

stanza (f). 'Room.' 'Adjoining rooms' are *stanze contigue. Stanza da letto* is 'bedroom', *stanza da pranzo* is 'dining-room', and *stanza da bagno* is 'bathroom'. *Il salotto* is 'the front room', 'sitting room', 'drawing room', or whatever you like to call it.

stare. This is one of the first verbs you have to study thoroughly, and you will be aware of most of the usual expressions, no doubt. Here are some of them: *stare buono*, 'to be good' (speaking of behaviour); *stare attento*, 'to pay attention'; *stare a suo agio, a disagio*, 'to be at one's ease, feel uncomfortable'; *stare a letto*, 'to be in bed'; *stare in piedi*, 'to be standing'; *stare per fare una cosa*, 'to be about to do something'; and so on. *Come state?* is 'How are you?' *Sto bene* is 'Well, thank you'. *Ti* (or *gli* or *le*) *sta bene!* means 'Serves you right!' One last note—if someone says *Sta zitto!* to you, you are being told to 'Shut up!'

stenografia (f). 'Shorthand' (*v.* OFFICE). A 'shorthand typist' is *stenodattilografa* (f).

stile (m). 'Style.' *Stile libero* in swimming is 'freestyle' or 'crawl' (*v.* SPORT).

stirare. 'To iron.' The 'iron' is *ferro* (*da stiro*) (*v.* HOUSEHOLD).

straccio (m). The general word for 'rag', 'cloth', 'duster'. You may also hear someone referred to as *uno straccio*, which isn't very polite, and indicates that after his night on the tiles perhaps, he looks 'washed out', like a 'rag'.

strappare. This verb gives the idea of violently pulling something away from somewhere, and may be translated variously 'snatch', 'wrench', 'pull off', 'pull away', and so on. I include it, as you hear it quite frequently, although learners tend to ignore it for some reason, in favour of *prendere* or *tirare*.

stufa (f). 'Stove', 'heater'. *Stufa elettrica* is 'electric fire'.

stufato, stufo. The most common way of saying that you are fed up. *Sono stufo di aspettare qui, senza fare niente* is 'I'm fed up with waiting here, doing nothing'. The corresponding verb is *stufarsi*, 'to get fed up, be sick of something'. You can be *stufo* or *stufato* with something, while the thing itself is *seccante, scocciante* or *noioso* to you.

Uno stufato is 'a stew' (*v.* FOOD).

stuoino (m). 'Mat' (*v.* HOUSEHOLD).

stupidaggine (f). 'Stupidity', 'stupid thing', 'stupid action'; 'nonsense', 'rubbish', 'rot'. Also 'a mere trifle'.

su. The point of mentioning this word is to draw attention to its use as an interjection. You wouldn't perhaps imagine it to be of very frequent use judging by usual dictionary entries such as 'Courage!' 'Bear up!' and so on. However, it *is* much used. In English we should usually say 'Come on', 'Come along' or 'Go on'. *Su* is used to encourage, much in the same way as *Dai*, although *Su* is somewhat gentler. Parents use it a lot in talking to their children. *Su, cammina, su* means 'Come along, walk, come on'. Animals are encouraged to take offered food from you, for example, by your saying *Su*. You encourage words from a hesitant mouth by saying *Su*. Some-times you may add another word to vary things. *Su, forza*, for instance. A quiz-master, met with dead silence on asking a question, could use *Su* to try to get an answer. *Forza* would be somewhat stronger (in fact, it is used more to encourage someone who is beginning to wilt).

Note also the expression *su per giù*, meaning 'approximately'. *Era su per giù la stessa passeggiata che aveva fatta il sabato*, 'It was just about the same walk he'd had on Saturday'.

subito. This almost always means 'at once', 'immediately', 'right away'. *Subito dopo* means 'directly afterwards'. Remember the emphasis on the first syllable, as opposed to the emphasis on the past participle of *subire* (to undergo), which is also written *subito* but accented on the middle syllable. *Vengo subito* should mean 'I'm just coming', 'I'll be with you directly', and it does mean just this, if you have it from the right person. If you are dubious about it when someone promises to come *subito*, you could repeat it, *subito subito*, to emphasize that it's important.

successo (m). This can be a masculine noun or the past participle of the verb *succedere* (to happen, to ensue). The noun means 'success'; *senza successo* is 'without any success'. The main meaning of the verb form is *è successo* 'has happened'. *Cosa è successo?* means 'What's happened?'

sugo (m). 'Gravy', 'juice' (*v.* FOOD).

suonare. 'To sound.' When you hear something that doesn't sound right or very pleasant, you say *Non suona bene*.

susina (f). 'Plum' (*v.* FOOD).

svelto. This adjective means 'quick', 'nimble' or 'smart'. The order *Via, svelto* means 'Make it snappy', 'Be quick about it'.

sviluppo (m). 'Development.' The verb is *sviluppare*. The word is also used for photography. *Sviluppo e stampa* is 'developing and printing'.

svolgere. This verb also means 'to develop', but in a somewhat different sense. *Come si sono svolte le cose?* ——'How did things turn out?' Physical development is, of course, *sviluppo* (*q.v.*), from the verb *sviluppare*, while *svolgere* gives the idea of events developing. In industry, you carry out programmes, and the verb used here is *svolgere*.

T

tabaccaio (m). 'Tobacconist', 'tobacconist's' (*v.* SHOPS).

tacchino (m). 'Turkey' (*v.* FOOD).

tachimetro (m). 'Speedometer' (*v.* CARS).

tagliacarte (m). 'Paper-knife' (v. OFFICE). This word comes from the verb *tagliare*, quite simple and meaning 'to cut'. The snag is that *tagliare* is so easily confused with *togliere* (q.v.), meaning 'to take off' etc.

tanto. *Di tanto in tanto* means 'from time to time'. *Ogni tanto* is 'now and then'. *Tanto meglio/peggio per lui* means 'All the better/worse for him'. *Tanta gente* is 'so many people'. *Mio fratello mangia tanto* is 'My brother eats such a lot'. *Il signor X è tanto buono* means 'Mr. X is such a good man'. When someone takes leave of another person, he often uses the expression *Tante cose*, which is really a short form of *Tante belle cose*, 'So many beautiful things' (which he hopes will come to you). Returning a greeting, *Altrettanto* means 'The same to you'.

One more thing about *tanto*. In a bus, for example, you might hear someone say *Si accomodi, signora*, offering a lady his seat (mind you, you'd have to choose your bus route very carefully to have a chance of finding an example of this!). The lady, perhaps hesitant of accepting, may be slow to sit, whereupon the offerer could say *Prego, si accomodi . . . tanto io scendo subito*, 'Please sit down, as I'm getting off soon, anyway'. In this way it's a shortened form of *tanto più che*, meaning 'especially as', or 'seeing that'.

tappeto (m). 'Carpet' (v. HOUSEHOLD).

tappezzeria (f). 'Upholstery' (v. CARS).

tappo (m). 'Stopper', 'plug' (v. HOUSEHOLD). This is what the dictionary might or might not, but in any case should, tell us. In fact, there is the other meaning in colloquial Italian of 'a short person', 'shortie'. *È un tappo* means 'He's very short', 'He's undersized'.
Tappo del radiatore is 'radiator cap' (v. CARS).

targa (f). 'Number plate' (v. CARS). The adjective is *targata*.

tastiera (f). 'Keyboard' (of piano or typewriter). One key is called *un tasto* (v. OFFICE).

tavola, tavolo (f, m). 'Table', one of the words that can be either masculine or feminine. *Tavola calda* refers to 'delicatessen' and, as you may eat there, it can also be translated 'snack bar'.

teglia (f). 'Pan' (v. HOUSEHOLD).

tegola (f). 'Roof tile' (v. HOUSEHOLD).

teiera (f). 'Teapot' (v. HOUSEHOLD).

telaio (m). 'Frame', 'chassis' (v. CARS).

televisore (m). 'Television set' (v. HOUSEHOLD). 'To see something on television' is *vedere alla televisione*.

tendina (f). 'Curtain' (v. HOUSEHOLD).

tenuta (f) **di olio.** 'Oil seal' (*v.* CARS). *A tenuta d'acqua, a tenuta d'aria* and *a tenuta d'olio* are respectively 'water-tight', 'air-tight' and 'oil-tight'.

tergicristallo (m). 'Windscreen-wiper' (*v.* CARS).

terraglia (f). 'Earthenware' (*v.* HOUSEHOLD).

terzino (m). 'Back' (in football) (*v.* SPORT). The two backs are, of course, *terzino destro* and *terzino sinistro*.

testa (f). 'Head', also when calling 'heads or tails', *testa o croce? Testa (di biella)* is the 'big-end' in an engine. 'Cylinder head' is *testata* or else *testa cilindro* (*v.* CARS). *Testa nucleare* is 'nuclear warhead'.

tifoso (m). 'Supporter', 'fan' (*v.* SPORT). *Un tifoso di Alberto Rossi* is 'a fan of Alberto Rossi'. *Fare il tifo* is 'to support', in sport, at least. (Although *tifo* is really 'typhus'.)

timbro (m). *Timbro postale* is 'postmark' (*v.* OFFICE). *Un timbro di gomma* is 'a rubber stamp'.

tintarella (f). This is a diminutive deriving from *tinta*, 'colour', 'hue'. It is used in the following way: *Durante le vacanze ho preso un po' di tintarella* meaning 'During the holidays I have got a bit of suntan'. It's a word often heard at the beginning of the season for taking the sun.

tizio (m). 'Individual', 'fellow', 'chap'. The feminine is *tizia*. *Stava parlando con un tizio all'ingresso* means 'He was talking to some chap at the door'. Naturally the word has a slight pejorative flavour, but nothing to be alarmed about, and it is widely used.

toccare. 'To touch.' In music, *e.g. toccare il pianoforte*, it is 'to play' although *suonare* is the usual verb for most instruments. Intransitively, it means 'to be up to', 'to concern' and so on. *Tocca a lui fare questo* means 'It's up to him to do this'. *Tocca a me* is 'It's my go, my turn'.

togliere. The básic meaning here is 'to take something away'. You can use the verb with a variety of meanings, in fact, such as 'to dissuade' (to take away the desire), or 'to steal' (to take away without permission). *Togliersi la sete* is 'to quench one's thirst', and likewise *togliersi la fame* is 'to stay one's hunger'.
　　Apart from this, there is the construction *Ciò non toglie che* . . . (plus subjunctive) meaning 'That doesn't stop . . . from . . .'. For example: *Ciò non toglie che lei lo dica*, 'That doesn't stop her from saying it'. The imperative form is *tolga*, as in: *Si tolga il cappello*,'Take your hat off'. Note the common question: *Mi toglie una curiosità?*, 'Would you mind telling me something (which I'm curious about)?' Lastly: suicides are often reported these days, and in Italian papers are often worded thus: *X si è tolto la vita la notte scorsa*, 'X took his life last night'.

tonno (m). 'Tunny' (v. FOOD).

torrefazione (f). 'Coffee roaster's' (v. SHOPS). Well, not only coffee, but this is the most important ware.

torta (f). 'Cake' (v. FOOD).

traguardo (m). 'Tape', 'finishing line' (v. SPORT).

tramontana (f). 'North wind' or 'north-east wind'. Rome gets this cold wind occasionally from late autumn onwards.

tramonto (m). This word is included, as it looks rather improbable for 'sunset', and usually escapes learners when they want to include it in a sentence. *Al tramonto* means 'at sunset'. 'From sunrise to sunset' is *dall'alba al tramonto*. Note that *tramonto* is not necessarily 'sunset', as it means 'setting' or 'going down' in general. For example, it is also possible to say *il tramonto della luna*.

trampolino (m). 'Spring-board', 'diving-board' (v. SPORT).

trasmissione (f). 'Broadcast' (radio). Also 'transmission' (v. CARS).

tratto d'unione (m). 'Hyphen' (v. OFFICE). *A un tratto* is 'suddenly'. *Tutto a un tratto* emphasizes this idea.

trattoria (f). Restaurant, less imposing than those called *ristoranti*. The less central ones, tending also to be cheaper, usually have specialities for each day, which almost everyone eats. Thursday, for example, sees the serving of *gnocchi*, a sort of shell-shaped potato dish, each *gnocco* being about the size of a penny. They are boiled and served with a tomato and cheese mixture.

tredicesimo. This is the ordinal number 'thirteenth', but in its feminine form generally refers to the 'thirteenth month', which Italian employers have to pay their employees for every year. Call it 'Christmas bonus', if you like.

tremendo. This means 'tremendous' in the sense of 'very large'. But the common colloquial meaning of the word may trip you up, as it's a false friend. If, for instance, you are waiting by the water's edge wondering whether or not to take the plunge, as you are afraid the temperature of the water may be rather on the low side, and you ask a person coming out of the water what it's like, he may well say to you *È tremendo!* In this case it would be wiser to stay dry, as the Italian idea is 'tremendously bad', rather than the usual English idea of 'tremendously good'. *Una cosa tremenda* is therefore 'a terrible thing'.

tromba (f). 'Trumpet.' Of a car, 'horn' (v. CARS).

trota (f). 'Trout' (v. FOOD).

tubo (m). 'Tube', 'pipe' or 'hose'. *Tubo di scappamento* is 'exhaust pipe' (v. CARS).

tuffarsi. 'To dive' (v. SPORT).

U

ubriaco. The usual word for 'drunk'. As in other languages, Italian has a multiplicity of adjectives for this state, most of them rather slangy (*sbronzo come una cucuzza*, for instance), but *ubriaco* is a good general-purpose word.

uccelleria (f). Literally, 'bird-shop' (v. SHOPS). Actually, in my nearest *uccelleria* there are several pups, at least two kittens, numerous tiny tortoises and some hamsters, apart from a great assortment of tiny birds and some larger ones. Therefore I refer to such shops as 'pet shops', not restricting the name to birds.

uccidere. The usual word meaning 'to kill', and which nearly always slips learners' memories. The other common word for 'to kill' is *ammazzare.*

udire. This verb, as you know, is full of irregularities, but this should not trouble you unduly, particularly as the verb for 'to hear' in almost universal use is *sentire* (q.v.).

ufficio (m). 'Office.' 'Post Office' is *Ufficio Postale. Ufficio cassa* is 'cash office' (v. OFFICE).

ultimamente. This does not mean 'ultimately', which is *finalmente*, but 'recently, of late, lately'. Therefore a very useful word. It may also mean 'lastly'.

umore (m). This is the usual word for 'mood' or 'temper'. *Essere di buon umore* is 'to be in a good mood'. *È di cattivo umore* is 'He's feeling bad-tempered, he's in a bad mood'.

undici. The number 'eleven', referring in the apposite context to a football team, just as we in English refer to a cricket or football team as 'an eleven'.

unico. One and only, single, sole. *Un figlio unico* is 'an only son'. *È l'unico modo* means 'It's the only way'. If you see a road sign reading *Senso Unico*, you know that it's a one-way street.

uovo (m). 'Egg.' Remember the plural *uova. Un uovo sodo* is 'a hard-boiled egg'. 'A poached egg' is *un uovo affogato.* The 'yolk' is called the *tuorlo dell'uovo.* And always remember that *È meglio un uovo oggi che una gallina domani*, 'A bird in the hand is worth two in the bush'.

utensile (m). 'Tool' or 'implement'. Here are the names of some of the most common:
    chisel, *scalpello* (m)
    corkscrew, *cavatappi* (m)
    drill, *trapano* (m)
    file, *lima* (f)
    hacksaw, *seghetto a mano* (m)
    hammer, *martello* (m)

monkey wrench, *chiave inglese* (f)
nut and bolt, *dado* (m) *e vite* (f)
nail, *chiodo* (m)
pliers, *pinze* (f pl)
punch, *punzone* (m)
rasp, *raspa* (f)
saw, *sega* (f)
spanner, *chiave* (f)
screwdriver, *cacciavite* (m)
vice, *morsa* (f)

Perhaps 'nails, nuts and bolts' are not exactly 'tools' but it
seems logical to include them.

V

vaglia (m). The meaning I am concerned with here is 'money
order'. A *vaglia postale* is a 'postal order'. *Vaglia telegrafico*
means 'telegraph money order'.

vainiglia (f). 'Vanilla' (*v.* FOOD).

valere. 'To be worth', to be noted especially for the expression
valere la pena. Non vale la pena di imparare questa parola
means 'It's not worth learning this word'. *Questo film vale
la pena* is 'This film is worth seeing'.

valevole. A ticket (*biglietto*) may be *valevole*, that is, 'valid', for
a certain period (*fino a . . .*, 'until . . .'). The point I want to
bring out here is the use of the word in sport, when a boxer,
for example, fights for a title; the fight is *valevole per, i.e.*
'recognized as valid for', *il titolo*.

valigia (f). 'Suitcase.' *Fare le valige* is like the French *faire ses
valises*, 'to pack'. Some specialized shops have *Valigeria* on
their sign, which shows that they sell 'luggage'.

valvola (f). 'Valve.' In electricity it may be 'fuse'. *Una valvola
a due vie* is 'a two-way valve'.

vantaggio (m). 'Advantage.' In sport, the team that is leading
is *in vantaggio* (*v.* SPORT).

vasca (f). 'Basin' or 'bath-tub' (*vasca da bagno*) (*v.* HOUSEHOLD).

vaschetta (f). 'Little basin.' *Una vaschetta di pesci* is 'a fish-bowl'.

vassoio (m). 'Tray' (*v.* OFFICE). A 'tea-tray' is *vassoio del tè*.

vediamo. From *vedere*, 'to see'; this means, of course, 'Let's see'
or else 'We'll see'. Very frequently used when you have to
wait to see how something turns out: *Vediamo dopo*, 'Let's

see later on', or *Vedremo domani*, 'We'll see tomorrow'. *Ma vediamo un po'* gives the idea of 'But let's just have a look', 'Hang on a moment'. *Andiamo* and *speriamo* are the other two of the trio of *-iamo*'s, *andiamo* meaning 'come on', 'let's go', and so on, and *speriamo* or *speriamo bene* meaning 'let's hope so', 'let's hope for the best', and so forth. A fourth one to make it a quartet would be *facciamo*. *Facciamo così* is. 'let's do it this way', 'let's do this' etc.

vela (f). 'Sail.' 'A sailing ship' is generally *una nave*, while 'a yacht', if not called by the English name, is *una nave da diporto*. *Una barca a vela* is also 'a sailing boat'. A list of the sails would stretch from here to kingdom come, so suffice it to mention that the 'mainsail' is *vela di maestra*, the 'topsail' is *vela di gabbia* and 'mizzen sail' *vela di mezzana*. In sports papers, the sport of yachting or sailing is usually referred to simply as *vela*.

venire. 'To come.' This verb is straightforward and, although very much used, there is little that need be pointed out here. Don't mispronounce it and say *Venere*, as this is 'Venus' (with the accent on the first syllable). One useful expression is as exemplified in this sentence: *Cosa ti viene in mente?* meaning 'Whatever do you think you're doing?' or 'What's come over you?' or some such question, according to the circumstances.

ventilatore (m). 'Fan.' *Ventilatore elettrico* is 'electric fan' (*v.* CARS).

verde (m). The adjective means, of course, 'green'. *Essere al verde* is 'to be flat broke, to be skint'. *See also* **secco**.

verdura (f). In the plural, 'vegetables' or 'greens' (*v.* FOOD).

vergogna (m). *Avere vergogna* is 'to be ashamed'. *È una vergogna* is 'It's a shame', although the voice usually indicates that it 'is a crying shame', no less. Sometimes, perhaps, the best rendering of it would be 'There ought to be a law against it!' as in English we almost automatically revert to the law. *Quella ragazza non sente vergogna* means 'That girl has no sense of shame'.

verificare. Something of a false friend, as it usually means 'to check', 'to examine'. And *verificarsi* is 'to take place', usually used in the past . . . *si verificò ieri*, '. . . took place yesterday'. *Verificare la contabilità* is 'to audit the accounts'. 'To verify' is almost always *controllare*.

vero. Here's a refreshing thought. While Italians and others have to struggle with the dozens and dozens of variations (of grammar, form and intonation) of our question-tag system ('Nice day, isn't it?' 'You will come, won't you?' 'You had a lot of trouble, didn't you?' 'You had to do it, hadn't you?' 'I'm here, aren't I?'—these just to remind you of the complexity of them) we, on the other hand, to pick up the Italian system have only to learn *Non è vero?* which is sometimes shortened to *Vero? Fa caldo, non è vero?* is 'It's hot, isn't it'? Be careful, and don't overdo this construction. Italians use it quite a lot, but not so freely as we do in English.

Note also that *per dire il vero* means 'to tell the truth', just as *per dire la verità* does.

vetraio (m). 'Glazier' (*v.* SHOPS). *Una vetrina* is 'a display window'. *Vetro* is, of course, 'glass' (but not 'a glass', out of which you drink, which is *un bicchiere*). *Vetro* may also be 'window pane'. 'Frosted glass' is *vetro martellato* and 'fibre glass' is *fibra di vetro*.

via (f). As the name of a road in a town, *via* is 'road', as in *Via Flaminia*. If there is no proper name, there is the defining *di* when you use *via*, as a rule. 'Roadway', for example, is *via di transito*. According to the exact expression used, *via* may be 'way', 'road', 'route' and other things. Remember, however, that there are other words, especially *strada*. 'The Rule of the Road', for instance, is *Il Codice della Strada*. If a road is divided into 'lanes', these are called *corsie* (f). Where one road crosses another, there is *una crocevia*. A main road of importance is referred to as an *autostrada*. *Cammino* is another word to cope with, meaning, as you may realize, more the way you are going than the road you are walking along. Sometimes you see the word *vicolo*, which refers to a 'narrow street', 'lane'.

Here are a number of set expressions using *via*:

> *via d'uscita*, way of escape
> *Via Lattea*, The Milky Way
> *via senza uscita*, dead end
> *via cieca*, blind alley
> (*per*) *via aerea*, (by) air mail
> *la Via Appia*, The Appian Way

Note that a *viale* (m) is a broader, tree-lined road, an 'avenue'. A *largo* is also broad, but rather resembles a *piazza*.

As a noun, *via* has alternative meanings. On a ship, *una via d'acqua* is 'a leak'. Then we have the expression *vie di fatto*, 'blows' or 'assault and battery'. *Loro sono venuti a vie di fatto* means 'They came to blows'. And 'legal steps' are *vie giudiziarie*.

Via also has great use as an adverb, meaning 'away', 'off'. *Andare via* is 'to go away', like *andarsene*. You may say *Vado via* just as you may say *Me ne vado*. 'To throw something away' is *buttare via qualche cosa*. *Mandare via* is 'to order off'. If you want someone to go away, you say *Via!* (or the longer forms *Andate via!* or *Va' via!*). If you are pestered by a dog (which, by the way, is far less likely in Italy than in England, firstly because there are fewer dogs, and secondly because the law says that dogs in towns must wear muzzles—and they usually do, too), then you will try to get him to go away by calling out *Via!* The last point is to mention the expression *e così via*, meaning 'and so on, and so forth'. This you will hear very frequently, just as 'and so on' is so often used in English.

vincere. 'To win' (a competition, a race, a battle, *e così via*). *Vincita* (f) is 'win', 'victory' or 'winnings'. 'The winner' is *il vincitore*. *Battere* is 'to beat', although there is not the same clear-cut division between *vincere* and *battere* in Italian, as in English there is between 'to win' and 'to beat'. *Vincere* can, on occasion, be used where we use *battere*, with the meaning of 'overcome'. For example, we 'beat a competitor', while Italians can *vincere un concorrente*.

vino (m). Everybody knows that this is wine. It remains only to specify a few kinds. *Vino amabile* is 'sweet wine', as is also *vino dolce*. *Vino da tavola* is 'ordinary table wine'. 'White wine' is *vino bianco* and 'red wine' is *vino rosso*. 'Dry wine' is *vino secco* and *vino spumante* (or plain *spumante*) is 'sparkling wine'. You can buy wine all over the place, in cafés, bars, dairies and so on, apart from the shops marked *Vini, olii, liquori* (*v.* SHOPS). Note that most Italian wines are supposed to be bad travellers, so that they lose a lot of their special qualities if they are exported. Frascati wines, for example, can hardly do the half-hour journey to Rome without losing something.

virgola (f). 'Comma' (*v.* OFFICE). *Virgolette* (f pl) are 'inverted commas'.

visione (f). 'Vision.' In connexion with cinemas, you read of *prima, seconda* and *terza visione*. The category applies to the cinema, and you pay more for a *prima visione* than for the others. Prices are graded, although they do differ from cinema to cinema among those of the same category. The point is: if you want to see a film for half the price, or less, wait for it to leave the *prima visione* cinemas; although admittedly seats do get harder and the volume of sound does increase the further down the scale you go.

vite (f). 'Screw' (*v.* CARS). A 'screwdriver' is *cacciavite* (m). The 'thread' of the screw is called the *filetto*. 'To tighten a screw' is *stringere una vite*.

voglia (f). 'Desire', 'wish'. From the verb *volere*. *Voglia* often corresponds to the English 'feel like doing something', as, for example, in *Non avevo voglia di rispondere*, 'I didn't feel like answering'. Again, *Credi che non abbia voglia di prendere un caffè quando arriva?* 'Don't you think that she will feel like a cup of coffee when she arrives?' *Non ho voglia* means 'I don't feel like it'. *Avevo voglia di qualcosa di forte* is 'I felt like having something strong'.

volante (m). 'Driving wheel' (*v.* CARS).

volentieri. A very useful word to express your willingness to do
something. To accept with alacrity (or courtesy) you do it
volentieri, or else *con piacere*. *Volete accompagnarmi allo studio?*
—*Sì, ben volentieri* or *Grazie, volentieri*. ('Would you like
to come with me to the studio?' 'Yes, with pleasure' or
'Thank you, it's a pleasure.')

volere. The usual verb for 'to want'. Remember the subjunctive
after it if you use the construction *volere che . . .* verb. For
example, *Voglio che lei faccia così*, 'I want you to do it like
this'. Now let's have a look at the expression *ci vuole*. Usually
learners of Italian get hold of an obvious word and, finding
that it's possible to use it, always use it in a correct context,
never perhaps cottoning on to the fact that there is an alternative of more frequent occurrence. Such is the case with
the word 'necessary'. *Necessario* is certainly a good word to
use, sometimes the only one suitable in a given phrase. *Sì, è
assolutamente necessario* would be 'Yes, it's absolutely necessary'. However, there are two other ways to express the idea
of necessity, apart from using the verb *dovere*. These are—
using the word *bisogno* (*q.v.*) or the expression *ci vuole*. *Ci
vuole troppo tempo per fare una cosa simile* means 'Too much
time is necessary (required) to do such a thing'. *Ci vuole
pazienza* is 'Patience is called for'. *Cosa ci vuole qui?* asks the
question 'What's necessary here?' *Per imparare bene una
lingua ci vuole molta pratica* means 'In order to learn a language well, a lot of practice is needed'. You will by now have
realized, no doubt, that this construction means using a noun:
Ci vuole qualche cosa.

Notice that *ci vuole* is used in question form to ask 'how
long?' (*i.e.* 'how much time?') *Quanto ci vuole per andare alla
chiesa?* is 'How long does it take to get to the church?' *Ci
vuole molto tempo per il prossimo treno?* means 'Will it be long
till the next train?' And apart from this question form, you
may also put the answer in the *ci vuole* form. *Ci vuole almeno
una mezz'ora*, 'It'll be at least half an hour'.

Z

zoppicare. 'To limp', 'to be lame'. There is a saying that *chi va
con lo zoppo impara a zoppicare*. The dictionary tells us that
this is the same as the English 'birds of a feather . . . ', but this
is stretching the point somewhat. The sense of the saying is
that 'he who is apprenticed to a thief will become a thief himself'—perhaps not always 'thief', but something not quite
above board, at any rate.

zucca (f). 'Pumpkin' (*v.* FOOD).

zucchero (m). 'Sugar' (v. FOOD). 'Beet sugar' is *zucchero di barbabietola*, while 'sugar beet' is *barbabietola da zucchero*. 'Sugar cane' is *canna da zucchero*, and 'cane sugar' *zucchero di canna*. *Zuccheriera* is 'sugar-basin'.

zucchini (m pl). Vegetables, much used in the summer time, like small marrows. Often cut up and fried in oil, or scooped out and filled with minced meat.

zuppa (f). 'Soup.' Other words for 'soup' are *brodo* (broth), *minestra* and *minestrone* (vegetable soup) (v. FOOD).

SPECIAL VOCABULARIES

FALSE FRIENDS

There are very many words in English which have counterparts in Italian of exactly similar form, or very nearly so. Remember that we are speaking of the 'form' of the word, and not the meaning. In many cases also the meaning is similar, if not exactly the same, but this is not always the case, and it will pay you to be careful and check the meanings of all words when you first come across them, not being content to check only those of completely different form. Failing this there will be occasions when you will come unstuck. It is also worth mentioning that Italian, by its very nature, uses more words which to us in English are purely 'learned' words, or words used in a very restricted sense as against a general sense in Italian. Just look at the word *comporre*, in the expression *comporre il numero*, when you wish to dial a number. It is certainly stilted English to say 'compose the number' rather than 'dial the number'. *Una prova convincente è stata fornita ieri a Torino . . .* means 'Yesterday there was convincing proof in Turin. . . '. We could hardly say 'Convincing proof was furnished yesterday in Turin'. . . . And so on. However, in these cases it is a question of choosing another word to substitute for the one you immediately recognize as not suitable in English. Things are not always so straightforward, however, and below is a list of words called 'false friends', whose meaning is not immediately obvious in a sentence, and indeed may be very misleading. I must point out that this list has no claim whatever to being exhaustive.

Italian—English	*English—Italian*
accidenti, darn!	**accident,** incidente
accomodarsi, sit down	**accommodation,** alloggio
appuntare, sharpen	**appoint,** nominare
attaccare, stick, fasten	**attack,** attaccare, assalire
attendere, wait	**attend,** assistere
attico, penthouse	**attic,** soffitta
attuale, present	**actual,** vero, reale
attualmente, at present	**actually,** veramente, realmente
bar, coffee bar	**bar,** birreria, bar
bravo, clever, good	**brave,** coraggioso
cantina, cellar	**canteen,** ristorante (fabbrica ecc.)
commedia, play	**comedy,** commedia leggera
conferenza, lecture	**conference,** congresso

Italian—English

confezione, make, manufacture

controllare, check

controllo, check

critica, write-up, criticism

deluso, disappointed

diplomato, person with diploma

discreto, moderate

disgrazia, accident, mishap

educato, polite, well-mannered

emozione, excitement

eventualmente, possibly

fabbrica, factory

fabbricare, manufacture

fattoria, farm

geniale, of genius

ginnasio, high school

ignorare, not to know

largo, wide

lettura, reading

libreria, bookshop

magazzino, store, large shop

modello, model

morbido, soft, smooth

noioso, boring

occorrere, be necessary

ordinario, common, vulgar

paragone, comparison

patente, driving licence

pavimento, floor

petrolio, oil

pigione, rent

preventivo, estimate

procurare, get

pronto, hello; ready

raccomandare, advise; register (letter, parcel)

rimanere, become; remain

risultare, appear, prove to be

sangue freddo, calmness

scalpello, chisel

sciocco, silly

sensibile, sensitive

sentenza, judgment, sentence

signore, sir; ladies

English—Italian

confectionery, caramelle

control, controllare, dominare

control, autorità, influenza

critic, critico

delusion, illusione

diplomat, diplomatico

discreet, discreto

disgrace, vergogna

educated, istruito, educato

emotion, commozione

eventually, finalmente

fabric, tessuto

fabricate, inventare

factory, fabbrica

genial, cordiale

gymnasium, palestra

ignore, far finta di non vedere ecc.

large, grande

lecture, conferenza

library, biblioteca

magazine, rivista

model (lady), indossatrice

morbid, malsano, morboso

noisy, rumoroso

occur, succedere

ordinary, normale

paragon, modello perfetto

patent, brevetto

pavement, marciapiedi

petrol, benzina

pigeon, piccione

prevention, impedimento

procure, procurarsi

pronto, subito

recommend, consigliare, raccomandare

remain, rimanere

result, risultato

in cold blood, a sangue freddo

scalpel, bisturi

shock, scossa

sensible, sensato

sentence (gram.), frase; proposizione

Italian—English	*English—Italian*
simpatico, pleasant	**sympathetic**, compassionevole, comprensivo

DISCONCERTING GENDERS

As you know, most nouns ending in *-o* are masculine, while most ending in *-a* are feminine. You will have learned that *mano* and *radio* are the two exceptions to the first rule, while to the second rule there are the following exceptions:

names of men, professions and titles (*e.g. papa, dentista, poeta*)
nouns derived from Greek, ending in *-ma* or *-ta*: such as *poema, clima, diploma, pianeta*

It's a pretty safe bet that the gender of an Italian word which has the same form, or very nearly the same form, as the French or Spanish word, will correspond. This is, as I say, a very reasonable guide for those approaching Italian from either Spanish or French. However, you should never take things like this for granted whenever you have the opportunity of checking up. Occasionally you will come unstuck: 'blood', for example, *la sangre* in Spanish, is *il sangue* in Italian. And the capital of Sweden is *Estocolmo* in Spanish, whereas in Italian it is *Stoccolma.*

However, these points are not those which cause overmuch difficulty. The difficult ones are those words which exist in two forms, with an *-a* ending and with an *-o* ending, the two words having completely different meanings. Look at these lists in which I include the more important ones:

il ballo, dance	**la balla,** bale, bundle
il collo, neck	**la colla,** glue
il colpo, blow	**la colpa,** fault
il costo, cost	**la costa,** coast
il filo, thread	**la fila,** line
il fine, aim	**la fine,** end
il foglio, sheet (paper)	**la foglia,** leaf
il limo, mud	**la lima,** file
il manico, handle	**la manica,** sleeve **(La Manica,** the English Channel)
il mazzo, bunch (flowers)	**la mazza,** sledgehammer
il mento, chin	**la menta,** mint
il modo, manner	**la moda,** fashion
il porto, port	**la porta,** door
il punto, detail, dot	**la punta,** tip
lo spigo, lavender	**la spiga,** ear (corn)
il tasso, rate; badger	**la tassa,** tax
il velo, veil	**la vela,** sail, sailing

Nor is this all. There are also the following, which change gender in the plural (and I include here the nouns which have two different plurals, with different meanings):

il braccio	le braccia
il ciglio (eyelash)	le ciglia
il corno (horn)	le corna
il dito	le dita
il frutto	le frutta (i frutti are the fruits on the tree)
il ginocchio	le ginocchia
il labbro	le labbra
il lenzuolo	le lenzuola
il miglio	le miglia
il muro	le mura (city walls) (i muri, walls of a room)
l'osso	le ossa
il paio	le paia
il sopracciglio	le sopracciglia
l'uovo	le uova

Remember also that there are certain nouns which do not vary their form in the plural. You should know the following categories:

(a) nouns stressed on the last syllable, **la città, le città**
(b) monosyllabic nouns, **la gru** (crane), **le gru**
(c) nouns ending in a consonant, **il filobus, i filobus**
(d) composite nouns, **il portacenere, i portacenere**
(e) nouns ending in -*i*, **l'analisi, le analisi**

Up to now we have been thinking about the plurals of nouns. There are also a number of difficult points connected with the formation of the feminine. In the following list, the feminine is distinctly different from the masculine:

il babbo	la mamma
il bue	la mucca
il cane	la cagna
il fratello	la sorella
il genero	la nuora
il marito	la moglie
il maschio	la femmina
il padre	la madre
il re	la regina
l'uomo	la donna

There are others, but these are the most important, and although some of them are ridiculously easy, you would perhaps be surprised to hear how many times I have heard people who should know much better referring to *una fratella* and so on. Be on your guard.

It is worth making one other point, as so many people become confused when they are referring to animals ('But I don't want to say the feminine, I mean the male'). Names of animals ending in -*e* or -*u* usually remain the same for both masculine and feminine, **il tigre, la tigre.**

Some animal names have no feminine: **delfino, coniglio, topo, tordo** (thrush).

Some animal names have no masculine: **aquila, balena, pantera, rondine, scimmia, vipera, volpe.**

In the event of having to specify the masculine or feminine when the form is lacking, you say: either, for example, *la scimmia maschio* or *il topo femmina*, or else *il maschio della scimmia* or *la femmina del topo*.

Allow me to point out, in conclusion, what you have possibly already noted for yourself, that the main difficulty lies in differentiating between words having either gender snags or having just one letter different from each other. See, for instance, *capello* (hair) and *cappello* (hat), *dita* (fingers) and *ditta* (firm), *Marcello* (name) and *macello* (shambles).

CARS

Italian—English

acceleratore (m), accelerator

accendere il motore, to switch on the engine

accensione (f), ignition

accumulatore (m), accumulator

albero (m) a manovella, crankshaft

albero (m) di distribuzione, camshaft

ammortizzatore (m), shock-absorber

aria (f), choke

assale (m), axle

autista (m), chauffeur, driver

autorimessa (f), garage

avvisatore (m) acustico, hooter

batteria (f), battery

battistrada (f), tread

benzina (f), petrol

biella (f), connecting rod

blocco (m) cilindri, cylinder block

bobina (f), coil

bracciolo (m), arm-rest

bucatura (f), puncture

bullone (m), bolt

cacciavite (m), screwdriver

camera (f) d'aria, inner tube

candela (f), sparking plug

carburatore (m), carburettor

carter (m), crankcase

catena (f), chain

cavalli (m pl), horse-power

chiave (f), spanner

chiave dell'accensione, ignition key

chiave fissa doppia, double-ended spanner

chiave inglese, monkey wrench

cilindro (m), cylinder

cofano (m), bonnet

condensatore (m), condenser

conducente (m), driver

contachilometri (m), milometer, mileage indicator

coperchio (m), cover

copertone (m), tyre

coppa (f) dell'olio, oil sump

corrente (f), current

cric (m), jack

crocevia (f), crossroads

cruscotto (m), dashboard, panel

cuffia (f) radiatore, radiator grille

cuscinetto (m) a sfere, ball bearing

dado (m), nut

decarburare, to decarburize

differenziale (m), differential

dinamo (m), dynamo

di ricambio, spare

di riserva, spare, reserve

disco della frizione (m), clutch disc

distributore (m), distributor

fanale (m), headlight

fanali laterali, side lights

fanalino (m), lamp

fanalino rosso, rear light

far girare con la manovella di avviamento, to crank

faro (m), headlight

fermare, fermarsi, to stop

filo (m) di rame, copper wire

filtro (m) aria, filter, air cleaner

finestrino (m), window

forare, to puncture
foratura (f), puncture
forcella (f), fork
frenare, to brake
frenatura (f), braking
freno (m), brake
freno a mano, hand brake
freno a pedale, foot brake
frizione (f), clutch

ganascia (f) **del freno,** brake shoe
getto (m), jet
girare, to turn
giunto (m) **universale,** universal joint
gomma (f), tyre
grasso (m), grease
guasto (m), breakdown
guidare, to drive, to steer

incidente (m), accident
indicatore (m) **di direzione,** direction indicator
indicatore di velocità, speedometer
in folle, in neutral
ingrassaggio (m), greasing
interruttore (m), switch

leva (f), lever
liquido (m) **per freni,** brake fluid
lubrificatore (m), lubricator
lubrificazione (f), lubrication
luce (f) **posteriore,** rear light
lucidare, to polish
lunetta (f), rear window

macchina (f), car
magnete (m), magneto
maniglia (f), handle
maniglia porta, door handle
manovella (f), crank
manovella alzacristallo, window handle
marcia (f) **indietro,** reverse
martello (m), hammer
messa in marcia (f) **automatica,** self-starter

mettere fuori marcia, to put out of gear
mettere in marcia, to put in gear
molla (f), spring
motociclo (m), motor-bike
motore (m), engine, motor
mozzo (m), hub

oliatore (m), oil-can
olio (m), oil
olio lubrificante, lubricating oil

parabrezza (f), windscreen
parafango (m), mudguard
parasole (m), sunscreen
paraurti (m) **(anteriore, posteriore),** bumpers (front, rear)
parcheggiare, to park
parcheggio (m), car park, parking place
parcometro (m), parking meter
passaggio (m) **a livello,** level crossing
pedale (m), pedal
pendaglio (m), strap-handle
pericolo (m), danger
pinze (f pl), pliers
pneumatico (m), tyre
pompa (f), pump
pompare, to pump
portabagagli (m), trunk, rack
potenza (f), horse power
presa (f) **diretta,** top gear
proiettore (m), headlight
punto (m) **neutro,** neutral position

radiatore (m), radiator
riparazione (f), repair
riscaldatore (m), heating unit
ruttore (m), contact breaker

scappamento (m), exhaust
scatola (f) **del cambio,** gearbox
schienale (m), back of seat

scivolare, to slide, skid
scontro (m), crash, collision
scuola (f) guida, driving
  school
sdrucciolevole, slippery
sedile (m), seat
sedile (anteriore, poste-
  riore), seat (front, back)
segmento (m), piston ring
semiasse (m), axle-shaft
senza ingranaggi, gearless
serbatoio (m) del liquido dei
  freni, brake fluid supply
  tank
serbatoio benzina, petrol tank
silenziatore (m), silencer
sistema (m) di ingranaggi,
  gearing
slittare, to skid
slittata (f), skid
specchio (m) retrovisivo,
  rear-view mirror
spegnere il motore, to switch
  off the engine

spruzzatore (m), jet
stantuffo (m), piston

tachimetro (m), speedometer
tappezzeria (f), upholstery
tappo (m) del radiatore,
  radiator cap
targa (f), number plate
telaio (m), frame, chassis
tenuta (f) d'olio, oil seal
tergicristallo (m), windscreen-
  wiper
testa (f) cilindro, cylinder
  head
trasmissione (f), transmission
tromba (f), horn
tubo (m) di scappamento,
  exhaust pipe

valvola (f), valve
ventilatore (m), fan
vite (f), screw
volante (m), driving wheel

English—Italian

accelerator, acceleratore (m)
accident, incidente (m)
accumulator, accumulatore
  (m)
arm-rest, bracciolo (m)
axle, assale (m)
axle-shaft, semiasse (m)

back of seat, schienale (m)
ball bearing, cuscinetto (m) a
  sfere
battery, batteria (f)
bolt (and nut), bullone (m)
  (con dado)
bonnet, cofano (m)
boot, portabagagli (m)
brake, freno (m)
to brake, frenare
brake fluid, liquido (m) per
  freni
brake fluid supply tank,
  serbatoio (m) del liquido dei
  freni

brake shoe, ganascia (f) del
  freno
braking, frenatura (f), frenata
  (f)
breakdown, guasto (m), panna
  (f)
bumpers, paraurti (m)

camshaft, albero (m) di distribuzione
car, macchina (f)
carburettor, carburatore (m)
chain, catena (f)
chauffeur, autista (m)
choke, aria (f)
clutch, frizione (f)
clutch disc, disco (m) della
  frizione
coil, bobina (f)
collision, collisione (f)
condenser, condensatore (m)
connecting rod, biella (f)
contact breaker, ruttore (m)

copper wire, filo (m) di rame

cover, coperchio (m)

crank, manovella (f)

to crank, far girare con la manovella di avviamento

crankcase, carter (m)

cranking handle, manovella (f)

crankshaft, albero (m) a manovella

crossroads, crocevia (f)

current, corrente (f)

cylinder, cilindro (m)

cylinder block, blocco (m) cilindri

cylinder head, testa (f) cilindro

danger, pericolo (m)

dashboard, cruscotto (m)

decarburize, decarburare

differential, differenziale (m)

direction indicator, indicatore (m) di direzione

distributor, distributore (m)

door handle, maniglia (f) della portiera, maniglia dello sportello

double-ended spanner, chiave (f) fissa doppia

to drive, guidare

driver, conducente (m), autista (m)

driving school, scuola (f) guida

driving wheel, volante (m)

dynamo, dinamo (m)

engine, motore (m)

exhaust, scappamento (m)

exhaust pipe, tubo (m) di scappamento

fan, ventilatore (m)

filter (air cleaner), filtro (m) aria

fly wheel, volante (m)

foot brake, freno (m) a pedale

fork, forcella (f)

frame (chassis), telaio (m), chassis (m)

front bumpers, paraurti (m) anteriore

front seat, sedile (m) anteriore

garage, garage (m), autorimessa (f)

'gas', benzina (f)

gearbox, scatola (f) del cambio

gear lever, leva (f) del cambio di velocità

gearing, sistema (m) di ingranaggi

gearless, senza ingranaggi

to put into gear, mettere in marcia

to put out of gear, mettere fuori marcia

gears, ingranaggi (m pl)

grease, grasso (m)

greasing, ingrassaggio (m)

hammer, martello (m)

hand-brake, freno (m) a mano

handle, maniglia (f)

headlight, faro (m)

heating unit, riscaldatore (m)

horn, avvisatore (m) acustico, tromba (f), clakson (m)

horse-power, cavalli (m pl), potenza (f)

hub, mozzo (m)

ignition, accensione (f)

ignition key, chiave (f) dell'accensione

indicator, indicatore (m)

inner-tube, camera (f) d'aria

jack, cric (m)

jeep, jeep (f)

jet, getto (m), spruzzatore (m)

key, chiave (f)

lamp, fanale (m), fanalino (m)

level crossing, passaggio (m) a livello

lever, leva (f)
lid, coperchio (m)
lubricating oil, olio (m) lubrificante
lubrication, lubrificazione (f)
lubricator, lubrificatore (m)
luggage rack, portabagagli (m)

magneto, magnete (m)
mileage indicator, contachilometri (m)
milometer, contachilometri (m)
monkey wrench, chiave (f) inglese
motor, motore (m)
motor-bike, motociclo (m)
mudguard, parafango (m)

neutral position, punto (m) neutro
in neutral, in folle
number plate, targa (f)
nut, dado (m)

oil, olio (m)
oil-can, oliatore (m)
oil-gauge, manometro (m) dell'olio
oil seal, tenuta (f) d'olio
oil sump, coppa (f) dell'olio

panel (dashboard), cruscotto (m)
to park, parcheggiare
parking meter, parcometro (m)
parking place, parcheggio (m)
pedal, pedale (m)
petrol, benzina (f)
petrol tank, serbatoio (m) benzina
piston, stantuffo (m), pistone (m)
piston ring, segmento (m)
pliers, pinze (f pl)
to polish, lucidare
pump, pompa (f)

to pump, pompare
puncture, foratura (f), bucatura (f)
to puncture, forare, bucare

radiator, radiatore (m)
radiator cap, tappo (m) del radiatore
radiator grille, cuffia (f) radiatore
rear bumpers, paraurti (m) posteriore
rear light, fanalino (m) rosso, luci (f pl) di posizione
rear seats, sedili (m pl) posteriori
rearview mirror, specchio (m) retrovisivo
rear window, lunetta (f)
repair, riparazione (f)
reverse, marcia (f) indietro

screw, vite (f)
screwdriver, cacciavite (m)
seat, sedile (m)
self-starter, messa in marcia (f) automatica
shock-absorber, ammortizzatore (m)
sidelights, fanali (m pl) laterali
silencer, silenziatore (m)
skid, slittata (f)
to skid, slittare
spanner, chiave (f)
spare, di ricambio, di riserva
spare wheel, ruota (f) di scorta
spark plug, candela (f)
speedometer, indicatore (m) di velocità, tachimetro (m)
spring, molla (f)
to start up, mettere in marcia
to steer, guidare
steering wheel, volante (m)
to stop, fermare, fermarsi
strap-handle, pendaglio (m)
sun screen, parasole (m)
switch, interruttore (m)

to switch on, accendere il motore

to switch off, spegnere il motore

tail-light, luce (f) (di posizione) posteriore

'ticket', contravvenzione (f)

top gear, presa (f) diretta

transmission, trasmissione (f), cambio (m)

tread (of tyre), battistrada (f)

to turn round, girare

tyre, gomma (f), copertone (m), pneumatico (m)

universal joint, giunto (m) universale

upholstery, tappezzeria (f)

valve, valvola (f)

wheel, ruota (f)

window, finestrino (m)

window handle, manovella (f) alzacristallo

windscreen, parabrezza (f)

windscreen-wiper, tergicristallo (m)

wing, parafango (m)

THE HOUSEHOLD

Italian—English

accendere la luce, to put the
light on
acqua (f) potabile, drinking
water
ago (m), needle
ago da calza, knitting needle
armadio (m), cupboard
aspirapolvere (m), vacuum
cleaner

bagno (m), bathroom
barattolo (m), jar, tin
becco (m) a gas, gas jet
bicchiere (m), glass, tumbler
bidè (m), bidet
bollitore (m), kettle
bombola (f) di gas, gas
container
bottiglia (f), bottle
bucato (m), laundry, washing

cacciavite (m), screwdriver
caffettiera (f), coffee pot
candela (f), candle
caraffa (f), jug
cardine (m), hinge
carta (f) igienica, toilet paper
cassa (f), box
casseruola (f), saucepan
cestino (m), basket, waste
paper basket
chiave (f), key
chiodo (m), nail
coltello (m), knife
condotta (f), water pipe
contatore (m) (di gas, per
elettricità), meter (gas,
electricity)
coperta (f) di lana, (woollen)
blanket
cotone (m), cotton
cotone idrofilo, cotton wool
credenza (f), cupboard

cucchiaio (m), spoon
cucina (f), kitchen, kitchen
range, cooker
cucina elettrica, electric
cooker

ditale (m), thimble
doccia (f), shower-bath

elettricità (f), electricity

fare la maglia, fare la calza,
to knit
ferro (m) da stiro (elettrico),
(electric) iron
forbici (f pl), scissors
forbici per le unghie, nail
scissors
fornello (m) a gas, gas ring
fornello elettrico, electric
hot-plate
forno (m), oven
friggere, to fry
frigorifero (m), refrigerator

gabinetto (m), toilet, W.C.
gas (m), gas
guanciale (m), pillow

inserire la spina, to plug in
interruttore (m), switch

lampada (f), lamp, bulb
lampadina (f), bulb
lana (f), wool
lastra (f) di vetro, pane of
glass
lavabo (m), washbasin
lavandino (m), sink
lavare, to wash
lavatrice (f), washing machine
lenzuolo (m), sheet
letto (m), bed

luce (f), light
lucidatrice (f), floor polisher

manico (m), handle (of cup, tool)
maniglia (f), handle (of door)
manopola (f), knob
martello (m), hammer
mattonella (f), floor tile

nettapiedi (m), floor mat

padella (f), frying-pan
pala (f), shovel
pattumiera (f), dustbin
pavimento (m), floor
pentola (f), pot, casserole, kettle
piattino (m), saucer
piatto (m), plate, dish
pinze (f pl), pliers
piumino (m), feather duster
poltrona (f), armchair
pomello (m), knob
portacenere (m), ashtray
portalampada (m), bulb socket
presa (f), socket

quadro (m), picture

radazza (f), mop, squeegee
radio (f), radio, wireless
rasoio (m) **elettrico,** electric razor
riscaldamento (m) **centrale,** central heating
rondella (f), washer (of tap)
rubinetto (m), tap
rubinetto del gas, gas tap

scala (f), stairs, ladder
scaldabagno (m), geyser, water heater
scarico (m) **d'acqua,** water drain
scatola (f), box, tin
scolo (m), drain
scopa (f), broom
secchio (m), bucket
sedia (f), chair
sega (f), saw
servizio (m) **da tè,** tea service
seta (f), silk
spazzola (f), brush
spillo (m), pin
spina (f), plug (electric)
spolverare, to dust
stanza (f), room
stirare, to iron
straccio (m), rag, cloth, duster
stufa (f), stove (heater)
stufa elettrica, electric heater
stuoino (m), mat

tappeto (m), carpet
tappo (m), stopper, plug
tavola (f), **tavolo** (m), table
teglia (f), pan
tegola (f), tile
teiera (f), teapot
televisore (m), television set
tendina (f), curtain
terraglia (f), earthenware
tovaglia (f), tablecloth

vasca (f), basin
vaschetta (f), small basin, bowl
vassoio (m), tray
ventilatore (m) **elettrico,** electric fan
vetro (m), glass, window pane
vite (f), screw

English—Italian

armchair, poltrona (f)
ashtray, portacenere (m)

basin, vasca (f)
bathroom, stanza (f) da bagno, bagno (m)

bath-tub, vasca (f) da bagno
bed, letto (m)
bidet, bidè (m)
blanket, coperta (f) (di lana)
bowl, vasca (f), bacile (m)
box, scatola (f)

broom, scopa (f)
brush, spazzola (f)
bucket, secchio (m)
bulb (electric), lampada (f), lampadina (f)
bulb socket, portalampada (m)

candle, candela (f)
carpet, tappeto (m)
central heating, riscaldamento (m) centrale
chair, sedia (f)
cloth, straccio (m)
coffee-pot, caffettiera (f)
cotton, cotone (m)
cotton wool, cotone idrofilo
cup, tazza (f)
cupboard, credenza (f), armadio (m)
cushion, cuscino (m)

dish, piatto (m)
drain, scolo (m), tubo (m) di scarico
drain-pipe, scarico (m) di acqua
dustbin, pattumiera (f), secchio (m) delle immondizie
duster, strofinaccio (m)
dustpan, porta-immondizie (m)

earthenware, terraglia (f)
electric bulb, lampada (f), lampadina (f)
electric cooker, cucina (f) elettrica
electric fan, ventilatore (m) elettrico
electric fire, stufa (f) elettrica
electric hotplate, fornello (m) elettrico
electric iron, ferro (m) da stiro elettrico
electric plug, spina (f)
electric polishing machine, lucidatrice (f) elettrica
electric razor, rasoio (m) elettrico
electricity meter, contatore (m) per elettricità

feather duster, piumino (m)
floor, pavimento (m)
floor cloth, straccio (m)
floor polisher, lucidatrice (f)
to fry, friggere
frying-pan, padella (f)

gas, gas (m)
gas container, bombola (f) per gas
gas jet, becco (m) a gas
gas meter, contatore (m) del gas
gas pipe, condotta (f) del gas
gas ring, fornello (m) a gas
gas tap, rubinetto (m) del gas
geyser, scaldabagno (m)
glass, vetro (m)
glass (drinking), bicchiere (m)

hammer, martello (m)
handle, manico (m) (of cup, tool); maniglia (f) (of door)
hinge, cardine (m)

iron, ferro (m) (da stiro)
to iron, stirare

jar, barattolo (m), bottiglia (f)
jug, caraffa (f)

kettle, bollitore (m), pentola (f)

key, chiave (f)
kitchen range, cucina (f)
kitchen sink, acquaio (m)
knife, coltello (m)
knit, fare la maglia, fare la calza
knitting needle, ago (m) da calza
knob, manopola (f), pomello (m)

ladder, scala (f)
lamp, lampada (f)
light, luce (f)
to light, accendere (la luce)

mat, stuoino (m), nettapiedi (m)

meter, contatore (m)
mop, radazza (f)

nail, chiodo (m)
nail-scissors, forbici (f pl) per
le unghie
needle, ago (m)

oven, forno (m)

pan, teglia (f)
pane (of glass), vetro (m),
lastra (f) di vetro
pillow, guanciale (m)
pin, spillo (m)
plate, piatto (m)
pliers, pinze (f pl)
plug (stopper), tappo (m)
plug (electric), spina (f)
to plug in, inserire la spina
pot, pentola (f)

radio, radio (f)
rag, straccio (m)
refrigerator, frigorifero (m)

safety pin, spilla (f) di sicurezza, spilla da balia
saucepan, casseruola (f)
saucer, piattino (m)
saw, sega (f)
scissors, forbici (f pl)
screw, vite (f)
screwdriver, cacciavite (m)
sheet, lenzuolo (m)
shovel, pala (f)
shower, doccia (f)
silk, seta (f)
sink, lavandino (m)
socket, presa (f) (di corrente)
sofa, sofà (m)
spanner, chiave (f)

spoon, cucchiaio (m)
squeegee, radazza (f)
staircase, scala (f)
stove (cooker), cucina (f)
stove (heater), stufa (f)
switch, interruttore (m)
to switch off, spegnere (la luce)
to switch on, accendere (la
luce)

table, tavola (f), tavolo (m)
tablecloth, tovaglia (f)
tap, rubinetto (m)
teapot, teiera (f)
tea service, servizio (m) da tè
television set, televisore (m)
thimble, ditale (m)
tile (roof, wall), tegola (f)
tile (floor), mattonella (f)
tray, vassoio (m)
tumbler, bicchiere (m)

vacuum cleaner, aspirapolvere (m)

wardrobe, armadio (m)
washbasin, lavabo (m), lavandino (m)
washer (of tap), rondella (f)
to wash up, lavare
washing (laundry), bucato (m)
washing machine, lavatrice
(f)
waste paper basket, cestino
(m)
water (drinking), acqua (f)
potabile
water closet, gabinetto (m)
water drain, scarico (m)
d'acqua
water heater, scaldabagno (m)
water tap, rubinetto (m)
wool, lana (f)

FOOD

Italian—English

acciuga (f), anchovy
aceto (m), vinegar
acqua (f) minerale, mineral water
affumicato, smoked
agnello (m), lamb
aglio (m), garlic
albicocca (f), apricot
ananasso (m), pineapple
anitra (f), duck
antipasto (m), hors d'œuvres
aperitivo (m), aperitif
aragosta (f), lobster
arancia (f), orange
aringa (f), herring
arrosto (m), roast
asparago (m), asparagus

barbabietola (f), beetroot
bere, to drink
bevanda (f), drink
birra (f), beer
biscotti (m pl), biscuits
bistecca (f), beefsteak
braciola (f), chop
briciola (f), crumb
brodo (m), soup, broth
budino (m), pudding
burro (m), butter

cannella (f), cinnamon
carciofo (m), artichoke
carne (f) (macinata), meat (minced)
carota (f), carrot
cavolfiore (m), cauliflower
cavolini (m pl), Brussels sprouts
cavolo (m), cabbage
cena (f), supper, dinner
cetriolo (m), cucumber
cibo (m), food
ciliegia (f), cherry

cioccolata (f), chocolate
cipolla (f), onion
cocomero (m), water-melon
coniglio (m), rabbit
conto (m), bill
costoletta (f), chop
cotogna (f), quince
crema (f), cream, custard
crescione (m), cress
crosta (f), crust

dattero (m), date
dolce, sweet
dolci (m pl), dessert, sweets

fagiano (m), pheasant
fagiolo (m), bean (haricot)
farina (f), flour
fava (f), bean
fegato (m), liver
fetta, fettina (f), slice, rasher
fico (m), fig
filetto (m), fillet
formaggio (m), cheese
fragola (f), strawberry
friggere, to fry
frittata (f). omelet
frittella (f), fritter
fritto, fried
fungo (m), mushroom

gamberetto (m), shrimp
gambero (m), prawn
gelatina (f), jelly
gelato (m), ice-cream
ghiaccio (m), ice
granchio (m), crab
granchiolino (m), crayfish
groviera (f), Gruyère cheese

insalata (f), salad

lampone (m), raspberry
latte (m), milk

lattuga (f), lettuce
legume (m), vegetable
lenticchie (f pl), lentils
limone (m), lemon
lingua (f), tongue
lombata (f), **lombo** (m), sirloin

maiale (m), pork
maionese (f), mayonnaise
mandorla (f), almond
manzo (m), beef
marinato, pickled
marmellata (f), jam, marmalade
mela (f), apple
melone (m), melon
menta (f), mint
merluzzo (m), cod
midollo (m), marrow
miele (m), honey
minestra (f), soup
minestrone (m), vegetable soup
montone (m), mutton
mora (f), blackberry
mozzarella (f), mozzarella cheese

nocciola (f), hazel nut
noce (f), nut, walnut
noce moscata, nutmeg

oca (f), goose
olio (m) **d'oliva**, olive oil
oliva (f), olive
ostrica (f), oyster

pane (m), bread
panna (f), cream

parmigiano (m), Parmesan cheese
passerino (m), plaice
pasticcio (m), pie
pastinaca (f), parsnip
pasto (m), meal
patata (f), potato
pepe (m), pepper
pera (f), pear
pernice (f), partridge
pesca (f), peach

pesce (m), fish
piccione (m), pigeon
pisello (m), pea
pizza (f), pizza
pollo (m), chicken
pomodoro (m), tomato
pompelmo (m), grapefruit
porro (m), leek
pranzo (m), dinner
prezzemolo (m), parsley
prima colazione (f), breakfast
prosciutto (m) **(cotto, crudo)**, ham (cooked, smoked)
prugna (f), plum

radice (f), radish
rapa (f), turnip
ribes (m), currant
rinfresco (m), refreshment
ripieno, filled
riso (m), rice
rognoni (m pl), kidneys
rombo (m), turbot

salamoia (f), pickles
sale (m), salt
salmone (m), salmon
salsa (f), sauce, gravy
salsiccia (f), sausage
salvia (f), sage
sardina (f), sardine
scombro (m), mackerel
sedano (m), celery
senape (f), mustard, French mustard
seppia (f), squid
sidro (m), cider
sogliola (f), sole
spinaci (m pl), spinach
spremuta (f), squash (of fruit)
spumante (m), sparkling wine
spuntino (m), snack
stufato (m), stew
sugo (m), juice
susina (f), plum

tacchino (m), turkey
tonno (m), tunny
torta (f), cake
trota (f), trout

uova alla coque, boiled eggs
uovo (m) affogato, poached egg
uovo fritto, fried egg
uva (f), grape
uva secca, raisin
uva spina, gooseberry

vainiglia (f), vanilla
verdura (f), greens, vegetables
vino (m), wine

vino amabile, sweet wine
vino bianco, white wine
vino dolce, sweet wine
vino rosso, red wine
vino secco, dry wine
vitello (m), veal

zucca (f), pumpkin
zucchero (m), sugar
zucchini (m pl), small marrows
zuppa (f), soup

English—Italian

almond, mandorla (f)
anchovy, acciuga (f)
aperitif, aperitivo (m)
apple, mela (f)
apricot, albicocca (f)
artichoke, carciofo (m)
asparagus, asparago (m)

bacon, bacon (m), lardo (m) fritto
baked, (cotto) al forno
banana, banana (f)
bean (haricot), fagiolo (m)
bean, fava (f)
beef, manzo (m)
beefsteak, bistecca (f) (di bue)
beer, birra (f)
beetroot, barbabietola (f)
bill, conto (m)
biscuits, biscotti (m pl)
blackberry, mora (f)
boiled eggs, uova alla coque
bread, pane (m)
breadcrumbs, pangrattato (m)
breakfast, prima colazione (f)
butter, burro (m)

cabbage, cavolo (m)
cake, torta (f)
carrot, carota (f)
cauliflower, cavolfiore (m)
celery, sedano (m)
cheese, formaggio (m)
Dutch cheese, formaggio olandese
Gruyère cheese, groviera (f)

Parmesan cheese, parmigiano (m)
cherry, ciliegia (f)
chestnut, castagna (f)
chicken, pollo (m)
chocolate, cioccolata (f)
chop, cotoletta (f)
cider, sidro (m)
cinnamon, cannella (f)
clove, garofano (m)
cod, merluzzo (m)
crab, granchio (m)
crayfish, granchiolino (m)
cream, panna (f), crema (f)
cress, crescione (m)
crumb, briciola (f)
crust, crosta (f)
cucumber, cetriolo (m)
currant, ribes (m)
custard, crema (f) (al caramello)
cutlet, cotoletta (f)

date, dattero (m)
delicatessen, tavola (f) calda
dessert, dolci (m pl) e frutta (f pl)
dinner, cena (f), pranzo (m)
drink, bevanda (f)
to drink, bere
duck, anitra (f)

egg, uovo (m), pl. uova (f)

fig, fico (m)
fillet, filetto (m)

fish, pesce (m)
flour, farina (f)
food, cibo (m)
fried, fritto
fried egg, uovo (m) fritto
fruit, frutto (m), pl. frutta (f)
to fry, friggere

garlic, aglio (m)
goose, oca (f)
gooseberry, uva (f) spina
grapefruit, pompelmo (m)
grapes, uva (f)
grilled, arrosto (alla griglia, su la gratella)

ham (cooked, smoked), prosciutto (m) (cotto, crudo)
hard-boiled, duro
hazel nut, nocciola (f)
herring, aringa (f)
honey, miele (m)
hors d'œuvres, antipasto (m)

ice, ghiaccio (m)
ice-cream, gelato (m)
iced, ghiacciato

jam, marmellata (f)
jelly, gelatina (f)
juice, sugo (m)

ketchup, salsa (f) di pomodoro
kidneys, rognoni (m pl)

lamb, agnello (m)
leek, porro (m)
lemon, limone (m)
lentils, lenticchie (f pl)
lettuce, lattuga (f)
liver, fegato (m)
lobster, aragosta (f)

mackerel, scombro (m)
marmalade (orange), marmellata (f) (di arance)
marrow, midollo (m)

mayonnaise, maionese (f)
meal, pasto (m)
meat, carne (f)
melon, melone (m)
menu, menù (m)
milk, latte (m)
mince (minced meat), carne (f) tritata, carne macinata
mineral water, acqua (f) minerale
mint, menta (f)
mozzarella cheese, mozzarella (f)
mushroom, fungo (m)
mustard, senape (f), mostarda (f)
mutton, montone (m)

nut, noce (f)
nutmeg, noce moscata

olive, oliva (f)
olive oil, olio (m) (d'oliva)
omelette, omelette (f), frittata (f)
onion, cipolla (f)
orange, arancia (f)
oyster, ostrica (f)

pancake, focaccia (f)
parsley, prezzemolo (m)
parsnip, pastinaca (f)
partridge, pernice (f)
pastry, pasticceria; pasta (f)
pea, pisello (m)
peach, pesca (f)
pear, pera (f)
pepper, pepe (m)
pheasant, fagiano (m)
pickled, marinato
pickles, salamoia (f)
pie, pasticcio (m)
pigeon, piccione (m)
pineapple, ananasso (m)
pizza, pizza (f) (napoletana, con funghi, ecc.)
plaice, passerino (m)
plum, susina (f), prugna (f)

poached egg, uovo (m) affogato

pork, maiale (m)

potato, patata (f)

fried potatoes, patate fritte

prawns, scampi (m pl); gambero (m)

pudding, budino (m) (N.B. No exact equivalent can be given)

pumpkin, zucca (f)

quince, cotogna (f)

rabbit, coniglio (m)

radish, radice (f)

raisin, uva (f) secca

rasher, fetta (f), fettina (f)

raspberry, lampone (m)

refreshment, rinfresco (m)

rice, riso (m)

roast, arrosto

sage, salvia (f)

salad, insalata (f)

salmon, salmone (m)

salt, sale (m)

sardine, sardina (f)

sauce, salsa (f)

sausage, salsiccia (f)

scrambled egg, uovo (m) strapazzato

shrimp, gamberetto (m)

sirloin, lombata (f), lombo (m)

slice, fettina (f)

smoked, affumicato

snack, spuntino (m)

sole, sogliola (f)

soup (broth), brodo (m)

soup, clear, zuppa (f)

soup, vegetable, minestrone (m)

spaghetti, pastasciutta (f), *e.g.* fettuccine (f pl), cannelloni (m pl), spaghetti (m pl)

spinach, spinaci (m pl)

sprouts, cavolini (m pl) (di Bruxelles)

squash, spremuta (f) (di . . .

squid, seppia (f)

steak, braciola (f)

stew, stufato (m), ragù (m)

strawberry, fragola (f)

stuffing, ripieno (m)

sugar, zucchero (m)

supper, cena (f)

sweet, dolce (m)

tart, torta (f)

tea, tè (m)

tomato, pomodoro (m)

tongue, lingua (f)

trout, trota (f)

tunny, tonno (m)

turbot, rombo (m)

turkey, tacchino (m)

turnip, rapa (f)

vanilla, vainiglia (f)

veal, vitello (m)

vegetables, legumi (m pl) (beans, peas); verdura (f) (greens)

vinegar, aceto (m)

walnut, noce (f)

water-melon, cocomero (m)

wine, vino (m)

dry wine, vino secco

red wine, vino rosso

sparkling wine, spumante (m)

sweet wine, vino dolce, vino amabile

white wine, vino bianco

SHOPS, PROFESSIONS

Italian—English

abbigliamento (m), clothes shop, outfitters
albergo (m), hotel
anagrafe (f), registry office
antichità (f), antiques
arredamenti (m pl), furniture shop
autonoleggio (m), car-hire
autorimessa (f), garage

banca (f), **banco** (m), bank
barbiere (m), barber's
birreria (f), beer shop
bottega (f), shop

caffè-bar (m), bar
calzolaio (m), shoeshop
camiceria (f), shirt shop
cartoleria (f), stationer's
casalinghi (m pl), ironmonger's, household articles
commessa (f), (girl) shop assistant
Comune (m), Town Hall
cremeria (f), dairy

dentista (m), dentist
drogheria (f), general store

edicola (f), kiosk, bookstall
erbivendolo (m), greengrocer's

falegname (m), carpenter
farmacia (f), chemist's
fiori (m pl), florist's
fruttivendolo (m), greengrocer's

garage (m), garage
gelateria (f), ice-cream shop
gioielleria (f), jeweller's
guanteria (f), glove shop

idraulico (m), plumber's

latteria (f), dairy
libreria (f), bookshop

macelleria (f), butcher's
magazzino (m), store
merciaio (m), haberdasher's
mobili (m pl), furniture shop

negozio (m), shop

oculista (m), oculist
orologeria (f), watchmaker's, jeweller's

panificio (m), baker's
parrucchiere (m), hairdresser's
pasticceria (f), pastrycook's, bakery
pelletteria (f), leather goods
pellicciaio (m), furrier's
pensione (f), boarding-house, hotel

Questura (f), Police Station

ristorante (m), restaurant
rosticceria (f), restaurant, roast meat shop

sali e tabacchi (m pl), state salt and tobacco shop
salsamenteria (f), grocer's, delicatessen
sartoria (f), tailor's

tabaccaio (m), tobacconist's
tavola calda (f), delicatessen, restaurant
torrefazione (f), coffee roaster's
trattoria (f), restaurant

uccelleria (f), pet shop, bird shop
ufficio postale (m), Post Office

valigeria (f), bag shop
vetraio (m), glazier's
vini - olii - liquori (m pl), wine-shop

English—Italian

antiques, antichità (f pl)

bag shop, valigeria (f)
baker's, panificio (m), pasticceria (cakes) (f)
bank, banca (f), banco (m)
bar, caffè-bar (m)
barber's, barbiere (m)
boarding house, pensione (f)
bookshop, libreria (f)
bookstall, edicola (f)
butcher's, macelleria (f)

car-hire, autonoleggio (m)
carpenter, falegname (m)
chemist's, farmacia (f)
clothes shop, abbigliamento (m)
coffee roaster's, torrefazione (f)

dairy, latteria (f), cremeria (f)
delicatessen, tavola (f) calda, salsamenteria (f)
dentist, dentista (m)

florist, fiorista (m)
fruit shop, fruttivendolo (m)
furniture, arredamenti (m pl), mobili (m pl)
furrier's, pellicciaio (m)

garage, autorimessa (f), garage (m)
general store, drogheria (f)
glazier, vetraio (m)
glove shop, guanteria (f)
greengrocer's, erbivendolo (m), fruttivendolo (m)
grocer's, salsamenteria (f)

haberdashery, merciaio (m)
hairdresser's, parrucchiere (m)

hotel, albergo (m), pensione (f)
household articles, casalinghi (m pl)

ice-cream shop, gelateria (f)
ironmonger's, casalinghi (m pl)

jeweller's, gioielleria (f)

kiosk, edicola (f)

leather goods, pelletteria (f)

oculist, oculista (m)

pastrycook's, pasticceria (f)
pet shop, uccelleria (f)
plumber, idraulico (m)
Police Station, Questura (f)
Post Office, ufficio postale (m)

registry office, anagrafe (f)
restaurant, ristorante (m), trattoria (f), rosticceria (f), tavola (f) calda
roast meat shop, rosticceria (f)

salt and tobacco shop, sali e tabacchi (m pl)
shirt shop, camiceria (f)
shoe shop, calzolaio (m)
shop, negozio (m), bottega (f)
shop assistant, commessa (f)
stationer's, cartoleria (f)
store, magazzino (m)

tailor's, sartoria (f)
tobacconist's, tabaccaio (m)
Town Hall, Comune (m)

watchmaker's, orologeria (f)
wine shop, vini - olii - liquori (m pl)

THE OFFICE

Italian—English

archiviàre, to file
archivio (m), files
assegno (m), cheque

battere a macchina, to type
busta (f), envelope

calcolatrice (f), computer
cancellare, to rub out, cross out
capufficio (m), head of office
caratteri (m pl) letters
carta (f), paper
carta asciugante, blotting paper
carta carbone, carbon paper
carta da bollo, carta bollata, official paper, stamped paper
carta da imballaggio, packing paper
carta da scrivere, writing paper
carta intestata, letterhead
carta per ciclostile, duplicating paper
carta protocollo, foolscap paper
carta straccia, waste paper
cartolina (f) postale, postcard
cassa (f), cash desk
cassaforte (f), safe
cassetto (m), drawer
cassiere (m), cashier
centralino (m), telephone exchange
cestino (m), waste paper basket
clichè (m), stencil
comunicazione (f), communication, message
contabilità (f), accounting, accounts department

conto (m), bill
copia (f), copy
copialettere (m), duplicating machine

dattilografa (f), typist
dattilografare, to type
dettare, to dictate
dittafono (m), dictaphone
due punti (m pl), colon

elenco (m) telefonico, telephone directory

fattorino (m), messenger
fattura (f), invoice
fermaglio (m), paper clip
foglio (m), sheet of paper
forbici (f pl), scissors
fra parentesi (f pl) (mettere), in brackets (to put)

gomma (f), rubber
gomma da inchiostro, ink rubber

imbucare, to post
impiegato (m), clerk
inchiostro (m), ink
inchiostro di china, Indian ink
indice (m), index
indirizzo (m), address

leva (f) liberacarta, paper release lever
libro (m) di cassa, cash book, accounts book
lineetta (f), dash

macchina (f) da scrivere, typewriter

macchina stampa-indirizzi, addressing machine
matita (f), pencil
metro (m), ruler

nastro (m), typewriter ribbon

orario (m) **di ufficio,** office hours

pagare, to pay
parentesi (f pl), brackets
paragrafo (m), paragraph
pennino (m), pen nib
pratica (f), file, folder
puntina (f) **da disegno,** drawing pin, thumbtack
punto (m), full stop
punto (f) **e virgola,** semi-colon
punto interrogativo, question mark
punzonare, to punch
punzone (m), punch

raccogliere, to collect, put together
raccoglitore (m), hard-backed file
ragioniere (m), accountant
riga (f), line
rigatrice (f), ruler

sbarra (f) **spaziatrice,** space bar
scaffale (m) **da archivio,** filing cupboard
scheda (f), card (for index)

schedario (m), card index
scrivania (f), desk
scrivere a macchina, to type
sede (f), central office, head office
segretaria (f), **segretario** (m), secretary
segreteria (f), office, secretarial office
spago (m), string
spedire, to dispatch, send
spedizione (f), dispatch department
spicci (m pl), change, petty cash
spillo (m), pin
sportello (m), counter (window)
stenodattilografa (f), shorthand typist
stenografia (f), shorthand

tagliacarte (m), paper-knife
tastiera (f), keyboard (of typewriter)
tasto (m), typewriter key
telefono (m), telephone
timbro (m) **postale,** postmark
tratto (m) **d'unione,** hyphen

ufficio (m), office
ufficio cassa, cash office

vaglia (f), money order, postal order
vassoio (m), tray
virgola (f), comma
virgolette (f pl), inverted commas

English—Italian

accountant, ragioniere (m)
accounts, contabilità (f)
addressograph, macchina (f) stampa-indirizzi

bill, conto (m), fattura (f)
block letters, stampatello (m)

blotting paper, carta (f) asciugante

brackets, parentesi (f pl)
in brackets (to put), fra parentesi (mettere)

carbon paper, carta (f) carbone
card (for index), scheda (f)
card-index, schedario (m)
cash (money), spicci (m pl)
cash book, libro (m) di cassa
cash desk, cassa (f)

cashier, cassiere (m or f)
cash office, ufficio (m) cassa
cheque, assegno (m)
clerk, impiegato (m)
colon, due punti (m pl)
comma, virgola (f)
computer, calcolatrice (f)
copy, copia (f)

dash, lineetta (f)
desk, scrivania (f)
dictaphone, dittafono (m)
dictate, dettare
directory (telephone), elenco (m) telefonico
dispatch, spedizione (f)
to dispatch, spedire
drawer, cassetto (m)
drawing pin, puntina (f) da disegno
duplicating machine, copia-lettere (m)

envelope, busta (f)

file, pratica (f); raccoglitore (m)
to file, archiviare
the files, archivio (m)
filing cabinet, scaffale (m) da archivio
full stop, punto (m)

guichet, sportello (m)

headed paper, carta (f) intestata
head of office, capufficio (m)
hyphen, tratto (m) d'unione

index, indice (m)
Indian ink, inchiostro (m) di china
ink, inchiostro
ink-eraser, gomma (f) da inchiostro
inverted commas, virgolette (f pl)
invoice, fattura (f)

key (of typewriter), tasto (m)
keyboard, tastiera (f)

message, comunicazione (f), messaggio (m)
messenger, fattorino (m)

nib, pennino (m)

office, ufficio (m)
head office, sede (f)
office hours, orario (m) di ufficio

paper, carta (f)
paper clip, fermaglio (m)
paper-knife, tagliacarte (m)
paper release lever, leva (f) liberacarta
duplicating paper, carta per ciclostile
foolscap paper, carta proto-collo
letter paper, carta da scrivere
packing paper, carta da imbal-laggio
stamped paper, carta da bollo, carta bollata
waste paper, carta straccia
paragraph, paragrafo (m)
to pay, pagare
pencil, matita (f)
to pick up, raccogliere
pin, spillo (m)
to post, imbucare
postal order, vaglia (f)
postcard, cartolina (f) postale
postmark, timbro (m) postale
punch, punzone (m)
to punch, punzonare

question mark, punto (m) interrogativo

ribbon (typewriter), nastro (m)
rubber, gomma (f)
to rub out, cancellare
ruler, riga (f), metro (m), rigatrice (f)

safe, cassaforte (f)
scissors, forbici (f pl)
secretary, segretario (m),
  segretaria (f)
secretarial office, segreteria
  (f)
semi-colon, punto (m) e
  virgola (f)
to send off, spedire
sheet of paper, foglio (m)
shorthand, stenografia (f)
shorthand typist, stenodattilografa (f)
space bar, sbarra (f) spaziatrice
stencil, clichè (m)

telephone, telefono (m)
telephone exchange, centralino (m)
tray, vassoio (m)
to type, battere a macchina,
  scrivere a macchina, dattilografare
typewriter, macchina (f) da
  scrivere
typist, dattilografa (f)

waste paper, carta (f) straccia
waste paper basket, cestino
  (m)

SPORTS

Italian—English

ala (f) **(destra, sinistra),** wing (right, left)
allenare, to train
allenatore (m), trainer
arbitro (m), referee, umpire
atleta (m), athlete
atletica (f), athletics
attaccante (m), attacker
attacco (m), attack, forward-line
atterrare, to knock down
avversario (m), opponent

battere (ai punti, k.o., k.o.t.), to beat (on points, knock out, t.k.o.)
batteria (f), heat
borsa (f), purse

calciatore (m), footballer
calcio (m), football
calcio d'angolo, corner kick
calcio di punizione, free kick
calcio di rigore, penalty kick
campionato (m), championship
campione (m), champion
campo (m), field, ground, pitch
canottaggio (m), rowing
centravanti (m), centre-forward
centro (m) **mediano,** centre-half
ciclismo (m), cycling
ciclista (m), cyclist
colpire, to hit, punch
colpo (m), blow, punch
combattimento (m), fight, contest
coppa (f), cup

corse (f pl) **ippiche,** horse races
corsia (f), lane

dilettante (m), amateur
dorso (m), back stroke

fallo (m), foul
fallo di mano, handball (football)
farfalla (f), butterfly stroke
formazione (f), line-up

gancio (m), hook
gara (f) **(femminile, maschile),** event (ladies', men's)
giallorossi (m pl), Rome F.C.
giavellotto (m), javelin
giocare, to play
giocatore (m), player
giro (m), turn, tour, lap
Giro di Francia, Tour de France
Giro d'Italia, Tour d'Italie
gol (m), goal

in palio (m), at stake
in vantaggio (m), leading

k.o., knock out
k.o.t., technical knock out

lanciare, to throw
lancio (m), throw
lancio del disco, throwing the discus
lancio del giavellotto, throwing the javelin

138

lancio del martello, throwing the hammer
lancio del peso, putting the shot

maglia gialla (f), 'yellow jersey', leader of Tour de France
manubrio (m), handlebars
maratona (f), marathon
marcia (f), walk, walking
martello (m), hammer
massaggiatore (m), masseur
mediano (m), half-back
motorismo (m), motor racing

nazionale (m), international
neroverdi (m pl), Atalanta F.C.
nuotare, to swim
nuotatore (m), swimmer
nuoto (m), swimming

ostacoli (m pl), hurdles

palestra (f), gymnasium
palla (f), ball
pallacanestro (m), basketball
pallanuoto (m), water-polo
pallone (m), ball
pareggiare, to draw, to tie, to equalize
pareggio (m), draw
parità (f), tie, draw
partita (f), game, match
peso (m), weight, shot
peso gallo, bantam weight
peso leggero, light weight
peso massimo, heavyweight
peso medio, middle weight
peso mediomassimo, light-heavyweight
peso mosca, fly weight
peso piuma, feather weight
peso welters, welter weight
pista (f), track
portiere (m), goalkeeper
primato (m), record
professionista (m), professional, pro.

pugilato (m), boxing
pugile (m), boxer
punti (m pl), points

rana (f), breast stroke
ring (m), boxing-ring,
ripresa (f), round, half
riserva (f), reserve
risultato (m), result
rossoneri (m pl), Milan F.C.

saltare, to jump
salto (m) **con l'asta** (f), pole vault
salto in alto, high jump
salto in lungo, long jump
salto triplo, hop, step and jump
scattare, to sprint
scattatore (m), sprinter
scherma (f), fencing
secondo (m), second
segnare, to score
Serie (f) **A, B,** First, Second Division
siepi (f pl), cross-country race; steeplechase
sport (m) **invernale,** winter sports
squadra (f), team
squadra ospite, home team
stabilire (primato mondiale), to establish (a world record)
staffetta (f), relay race
stagione (f), season
stile (m) **libero,** freestyle, crawl

terzino (m) **(destro, sinistro),** back (right, left), fullback
tifoso (m) **(di),** supporter, fan (of)
traguardo (m), tape, finishing line
trampolino (m), spring-board, diving-board
tuffarsi, to dive

undici (m pl), eleven, team

valevole (per), valid (for)
vantaggio (m), advantage

vela (f), yachting, sailing
vincere, to win

English—Italian

N.B. Italian football teams are very often referred to by colour›
according to their jerseys. For example, Rome are known as the
giallorossi, Palermo as *i rosaneri*, Milan as *i rossoneri*, and Atalanta
as *i neroverdi*.

amateur, dilettante (m)
athlete, atleta (m)
athletics, atletica (f) (leggera)

back (football), terzino (m)
back stroke, dorso (m)
bantam weight, peso (m)
gallo
ball, palla (f)
basketball, pallacanestro (m)
to beat (on points), battere
(ai punti)
boxer, pugile (m)
boxing, pugilato (m)
boxing-match, combattimento
(m)
boxing-ring, ring (m)
breast stroke, rana (f)
butterfly stroke, farfalla (f)

centre-forward, centravanti
(m)
centre-half, centro (m)
mediano
champion, campione (m)
championship, campionato
(m)
competition, gara (f)
corner-kick, calcio (m)
d'angolo
crawl, stile (m) libero
**cross-country race, steeple-
chase**, siepi (f pl)
cup, coppa (f)
cycling, ciclismo (m)

discus throwing, lancio (m)
del disco
dive, tuffarsi
diving-board, trampolino (m)

division, serie (f)
draw, pareggio (m), risultato
(m) di parità
to draw, pareggiare

eleven (team), undici (m pl)
establish (a world record),
stabilire (primato mondiale)

fan (of), tifoso (m) (di)
feather weight, peso (m)
piuma
fencing, scherma (f)
field, campo (m)
first division, Serie (f) A
fly weight, peso (m) mosca
football (ball), palla (f)
football (game), calcio (m)
footballer, calciatore (m)
football field, campo (m)
forward, attaccante (m)
forward-line, attacco (m)
free kick, calcio (m) di punizione
freestyle, stile (m) libero

game, partita (f)
goal, gol (m)
goalkeeper, portiere (m)

half (first, second), ripresa
(f) (prima, seconda)
half-back, mediano (m)
hammer throwing, lancio (m)
del martello
handlebars, manubrio (m)
heat, batteria (f)
heavyweight, peso (m) massimo

high jump, salto (m) in alto
home team, squadra (f) ospite
hook, gancio (m)
hop, step and jump, salto (m) triple
horse racing, corse (f pl) ippiche
hurdles, ostacoli (m pl)

international, nazionale (m) (a player for Italy is 'un azzurro' (m))

javelin throwing, lancio (m) del giavellotto
jump, saltare

kick, calcio (m)
to kick, calciare
to knock down, atterrare
to knock out (one's opponent), battere (l'avversario) k.o.

lane, corsia (f)
(be) leading, (essere) in vantaggio (m)
left-back, terzino (m) sinistro
left-half, mediano (m) sinistro
left-wing, ala (f) sinistra
light-heavyweight, peso (m) mediomassimo
light weight, peso leggero
line-up, formazione (f)
long jump, salto (m) in lungo

marathon, maratona (f)
masseur, massaggiatore (m)
match, partita (f)
middle weight, peso (m) medio
motor racing, motorismo (m)

outside left, ala (f) sinistra
outside right, ala destra

penalty kick, calcio (m) *or* tiro (m) di rigore

pitch, lancio (m)
player, giocatore (m)
points, punti (m pl)
pole vault, salto (m) con l'asta
professional, professionista (m or f)
punch, colpo (m)
to punch, colpire
puncture, bucatura (f)
purse (boxing), borsa (f)
putting the weight, lancio (m) del peso

race (ladies', men's), gara (f) (femminile, maschile)
record, record (m), primato (m)
referee, arbitro (m)
relay race, staffetta (f)
reserve, riserva (f)
result, risultato (m)
right-back, terzino (m) destro
right-half, mediano (m) destro
right-wing, ala (f) destra
round, ripresa (f)
rowing, canottaggio (m)

sailing, vela (f)
score (a goal), segnare (un gol)
season, stagione (f)
second (boxing), secondo (m)
second division, Serie (f) B
to sprint, scattare
sprinter, scattatore (m)
stake (at), (in) palio (m)
to swim, nuotare
swimmer, nuotatore (m)
swimming, nuoto (m)

tape (finishing-line), traguardo (m)
team, squadra (f)
t.k.o., k.o.t.
tennis, tennis (m)
to throw, lanciare
tour, giro (m)
Tour de France, Giro di Francia

tour-leader, maglia (f) gialla
trainer, allenatore (m)

umpire, arbitro (m)
uppercut, uppercut (m)

valid, valevole

walking, marcia (f)
water-polo, pallanuoto (m)
weight, peso (m)

weight-putting, lancio (m) del
peso
welter weight, peso (m)
welters
to win, vincere
(be) winning, (essere) in
vantaggio (m)
winger, ala (f)
winter sports, sport (m) in-
vernali

TELEPHONES

Italian—English

abbonato (m), subscriber
apparecchio (m), apparatus
attaccare, to hang up, ring off

c'è . . . ? is . . . there?
centrale (f) **interurbana**, trunk exchange
centrale urbana, local exchange
centralino (m), telephone exchange
chi parla? who's speaking?
chiamare, to call
chiamata (f), a call
comporre il numero, to dial the number

dica! go ahead
disco (m), dial
distaccare, to cut off
distacco (m), cutting off

fare il numero, to dial the number

gettone (m), token coin (for public telephones)
girare il disco, to dial
guasti (m pl) **all'apparecchio**, breakdown

interrompere, to break into
interurbana (f), trunk call

messaggio (m), message
microfono (m), microphone

numero (m) **guasto**, number out of order
numero impegnato, number engaged
numero sbagliato, wrong number

occupato, engaged
ora (f) **esatta**, correct time

padiglione (m), earpiece
prenotare, to book
prenotazione (f), booking
pronto! hello!

riattaccare, to hang up, ring off
ricevitore (m), receiver
richiamare, to call back

sono io, speaking
staccare il ricevitore, to take the receiver off, lift the receiver
sveglia (f) **telefonica**, automatic alarm

telefonata (f), telephone call
telefono (m), telephone
tono (m) **acustico**, tone

vorrei parlare con . . ., I should like to speak to . . .

English—Italian

alarm, sveglia (f) telefonica
apparatus, apparecchio

to book, prenotare
booking, prenotazione (f)

breakdown, guasto (m)
to break into, interrompere

call, chiamata (f)
to call, chiamare

to call back, richiamare
correct time, l'ora (f) esatta
to cut off, distaccare

dial, disco (m)
to dial, comporre *or* fare il numero, girare il disco

earpiece, padiglione (m)
engaged, occupato

go ahead! dica!

to hang up, attaccare, riattaccare
hello! pronto!

I should like to speak to . . . , vorrei parlare con . . .
is . . . there? c'è . . . ?

to lift the receiver, staccare il ricevitore
local exchange, centrale (f) urbana

message, messaggio (m)
microphone, microfono (m)

number, numero (m)
number engaged, numero impegnato
number out of order, numero guasto

receiver, ricevitore (m)
to ring off, attaccare, riattaccare
to ring up, chiamare

speaking, sono io
subscriber, abbonato (m)

to take off the receiver, staccare il ricevitore
telephone, telefono (m)
telephone call, telefonata (f), chiamata (f)
telephone exchange, centrale (f), centralino (m)
token coin, gettone (m)
trunk call, interurbana (f)
trunk exchange, centrale (f) interurbana

who's speaking? chi parla?
wrong number, numero sbagliato (m)

ENGLISH—ITALIAN

Cross-reference Index

IMPORTANT NOTE: It is of the utmost importance to note that this is exactly what it says it is, namely a *cross-reference index*. This means that the Italian word against the English one is not at all sure to be a translation of it, or even a near equivalent—indeed, the two words may be dead opposites, or almost so. The whole idea is to indicate here under what word you should look in the main section of the book, the Italian-English part, to find a reference to or explanation of the English word or expression in question. Therefore tread with care in this section.

able, capace
abuse, corno
accelerator, acceleratore
accident, accidente, disgrazia
accommodate, accomodare
according to, secondo
accountant, ragioniere
accounting, contabilità
accumulator, accumulatore
actually, attualmente
address, indirizzo
administration, comune
advantage, vantaggio
agreement, accordo
aim, scopo
air, aria
airmail, via
airtight, tenuta
all right, andare, bene
all the better, tanto
all the same, ebbene, in-
  differente
all the worse, tanto
almond, mandorla
already, già
amateur, dilettante
amuse, divertirsi
anchovy, acciuga
and so on, via
answer, rispondere
antiques, antichità
anyway, modo, comunque,
  tanto, insomma
aperitif, aperitivo

apologize, scusarsi
apparatus, apparecchio
appear, risultare
appearances, figura
apple, mela
approximately, su, press'a
  poco
apricot, albicocca
argument, argomento
armchair, poltrona
arm-rest, bracciolo
army, esercizio
arrange, combinare, sistemare
arrive, arrivare
artful, furbo
artichoke, carciofo
ashamed, vergogna
ashtray, portacenere
asparagus, asparago
assist, assistere
assistant, commessa
at all, affatto, mica
at once, pronto, subito
athlete, atleta
athletics, atletica
atmospherics, scarica
attack, attaccare
attend, assistere
attic, attico
attract, attirare
audit, verificare
August Bank Holiday, Ferragosto
away, via

axle, assale
axle-shaft, semiasse

B.A. (degree), laurea
back, dorso, terzino
back of seat, schienale
bad mood, nero
bad show, figura
bad word, parolaccia
badly, male
bag, borsa
baker's, panificio
ball, palla
ball bearing, cuscinetto
bank, banca
barbed wire, filo
bargain, affare
barrel, fusto
base, fondo
basin, vasca
basket, cestino
basketball, palla
bathing station, stabilimento
bathroom, bagno
bath (tub), vasca
baton, staffetta
battery, batteria
be about, girare
be around, girare
be best to, convenire
be broke, secco
be careful, fare
be left, rimanere
be necessary, occorrere
be patient, pazienza
be sure to, raccomandare
be very near to, mancare
be warm, fare
bean, fagiolo
beat, battere
beautiful, bello
become, diventare, rimanere
bed, letto
beef, manzo
beer, birra
beet sugar, zucchero
beetroot, barbabietola
beg (you), prego
begin to, mettere
beginning, inizio

bidet, bidè
bill, conto
bird in the hand, uovo
biscuit, biscotti
bit, pezzo
black, nero
blackberry, mora
blanket, coperta
blimey! accidenti!
blind alley, via
block letters, caratteri
block of flats, palazzo
blotting paper, carta
blow, colpire
blows, via
boarding-house, pensione
bonnet (car), cofano
book, libro
booking office, sportello
bookshop, libreria
bookstall, edicola
boot (car), portabagagli
bore, scocciare
boring, noioso, seccante
borrow, prendere
boss, capo
bottle, bottiglia
bottom, fondo
box, cassa; scatola
boxer, pugilato
boxing, pugilato
boxing category, peso
(in) brackets, fra parentesi
brake, frenare
brake fluid, liquido
brake shoe, ganascia
brave, bravo
brazen, sfrontato
brazenness, faccia
bread, pane
breadcrumbs, pane
breakdown, guasto, panna
breakfast, prima colazione
breast stroke, rana
brick, mattone
bring, portare
broadcast, trasmissione
broom, scopa
brush, spazzola
B.Sc., laurea

buck up, sbrigarsi
bucket, secchio
bulb, lampada
bulb socket, portalampada
bump off, fare
bumpers, parabrezza
business, faccenda
but, ma, però
butcher's, macelleria
butter, burro
butterfly, farfalla
by the way, proposito

cabbage, cavolo
cabin boy, mozzo
cake, torta
calculating machine, calcolatrice
call girl, squillo
camshaft, albero
can't be helped, pazienza
can't help, meno
cancel, cancellare
candle, candela
cane sugar, zucchero
car, macchina
car hire, autonoleggio
carburettor, carburatore
card index, scheda
carefree, spensierato
careful, attenzione
carpenter, falegname
carpet, tappeto
carrot, carota
carry, portare
carry out, svolgere
case, caso
(in any) case, modo, comunque
cashier, cassiere
casing, cuffia
castor oil, olio
catch cold, raffreddore
catch fire, pigliare
catch hold, addosso
cauliflower, cavolfiore
cause, motivo
celery, sedano
cellar, cantina
centre-forward, centravanti

centre-half, centro mediano
chain, catena
chair, sedia
champion, campione
championship, campionato
change, cambiare; spicci; resto
change mind, idea
chap, tizio
charity, carità
chassis, telaio
chatter, chiacchierare
chauffeur, autista
check, verificare, controllare
checkmate, matto
cheeky, sfrontato
cheer up! dai!
cheerio, ciao
cheese, formaggio
chemist's, farmacia
cheque, assegno
cherry, ciliegia
chicken, pollo
chip, gettone
chisel, utensile
chocolate, cioccolata
chop, braciola
Christmas bonus, tredicesima
cider, sidro
cinnamon, cannella
clerk, impiegato
clever, bravo; furbo; spiritoso
closet, gabinetto; sgabuzzino
cloth, straccio
clothes brush, spazzola
clutch, frizione
clutch disc, disco
coach, pullman
coconut oil, olio
cod, merluzzo
cod liver oil, olio
coffee, caffè
coil, bobina
cold blood, sangue
collect, raccogliere
collision, scontro
colon, due punti
combine, combinare
come, venire
come along! su!
come in! avanti!

come into, ci
come on! sul
come to blows, via
comedy, commedia
coming shortly, imminente
comma, virgola
common, ordinario
comparison, paragone
competition, gara
composer, compositore
compositor, compositore
computer, calcolatrice
condenser, condensatore
conference, conferenza
connecting rod, biella
consequently, quindi
container, bidone, bombola
contest, combattimento
control, controllare
cooker, cucina
cop, poliziotto
copy, copia
corkscrew, utensile
cornet, cono
cotton, cotone
cotton wool, cotone
counter, gettone
(of) course, come
cover, coperchio
crab, granchio
crafty, furbo
crank, manovella
crankcase, carter
crankshaft, albero
crash, scontro
crawl, stile
crayfish, granchiolino
craze, mania
crazy, diventare; scemo
cream, panna; crema
crikey! accidenti!
crime, delitto
criticize, criticare
cross, croce
crossroads, crocevia
crossword puzzle, cruciverba
crumb, briciola
crust, crosta
crying shame, vergogna
cup, coppa

cupboard, credenza, sgabuz-zino
cunning, furbo
currant, ribes
current, corrente
curtain, tendina
custom-built, serie
cut, tagliacarte
cut out, piantare
cutlet, costoletta
cycling, ciclismo
cyclist, ciclismo
cylinder, cilindro
cylinder block, blocco
cylinder head, testa

dairy, latteria
dance, ballo
danger, pericolo
dark, buio
dash, lineetta
dashboard, cruscotto
date, dattero
dead-end, via
dead loss, bidone
decarbonize, decarburare
decide, decidersi
degree, laurea
delay, ritardo
delicatessen, tavola calda
dentist, dentista
depends, secondo
desire, voglia
desk, scrivania
dessert, dolci
detective film, giallo
dectective story, giallo
develop, svolgere
development, sviluppo
dictaphone, dettare
dictate, dettare
die, morire
different, diverso
differential, differenziale
din, chiasso
dining-room, stanza
dinner, pranzo
dip (exam), laurea
diplomat/ic, diplomatico

disappointed, rimanere, male
disappointment, delusione
disaster, disastro
discharge, scarica
discount, sconto
discover, scoprire
discreet, discreto
discus, lancio
discussion, discussione
disgrace, disgrazia
dish, piatto
dislike, dispiace
dispatch, spedire
display window, vetraio
dive, tuffarsi
diving-board, trampolino
division, serie
do, fare
do without, meno
doesn't matter, niente
don't bother, mancare
don't care, fregare, importare
don't exaggerate, bisognare
don't forget, raccomandare
don't know, non so
don't mention, niente, prego
don't worry, preoccupare
doorkeeper, portinaio
drain, scolo
draw, pareggio
drawer, cassetto
drawing pin, puntina
drawing room, stanza
dressing-room, spogliatoio
drill, utensile; forare
drink, bere
driver, conducente
driving licence, patente
driving school, scuola guida
driving wheel, volante
drunk, ubriaco
drunken feeling, sbornia
duck, anitra
duplicating machine, copia-
lettere
dust, spolverare
dustbin, pattumiera
duster, straccio
dustpan, pattumiera
dynamo, dinamo

each other, ci
early bird catches, pigliare
earn living, mozzicone
earthenware, terraglia
easy chair, poltrona
educated, educato
effrontery, faccia
egg, uovo
electric fire, stufa
electricity, elettricità
eleven, undici
emotion, emozione
employee, impiegato
engine, motore
enjoy, divertirsi
enter, entrare
envelope, busta
errand boy, fattorino
establish, stabilire
establishment, stabilimento
estimate, preventivo
even, pure, ancora
event, gara
eventually, eventualmente
ever, mai
examine, verificare
excellent, bene
excitement, emozione
excursion, gita
excuse me, permesso; dispiace; scusarsi
exercise, esercizio
exhaust, scappamento
exploit, sfruttare

fabric, fabbrica
fabricate, fabbricare
face, faccia
factory, fabbrica, stabilimento
fag-end, mozzicone
fagged out, fiacca
failure, fallimento
fair, giusto
fall, cascare
famous, notorietà
fan, tifoso; ventilatore
farm, fattoria
fat, grasso
favour, favore, piacere
fed up, stufato

feel like, voglia
fellow, tizio
female, femmina
fence, siepe
fencing, scherma
few, poco
field, campo
fig, fico
fight, combattimento
figure, figura
file, archiviare; utensile
filled, ripieno
fillet, filetto
film critic, criticare
filter, filtro
fine thing, roba
fire station, posto
firm, ditta
first aid, pronto
fish-bowl, vaschetta
fish, pesce
fit, giusto
fix, sistemare, accomodare,
   stabilire
flabbergasted, rimanere
flat broke, verde
flight engineer, motore
floor, pavimento
floor mat, nettapiedi
floor tile, mattonella
flop, disastro
flour, farina
flying saucer, disco
fog light, luce
folder, pratica
food, cibo
foolscap, carta
football, calcio
footballer, calciatore
for want of, mancanza
force, forza
forget, scordarsi
fork, forcella
fork out, sputare fuori
formation, formazione
forward, prepotente
frame, telaio
freckle, lentiggine
free gift, omaggio
freestyle, stile

frog, rana
from now on, poi
from time to time, tanto
frosted glass, vetraio
fry, friggere
frying-pan, padella
fundamentally, fondo
furnace, forno
furniture, mobile
furrier, pellicciaio
fuse, valvola
fussy, pignolo

game, partita
garage, autorimessa
garlic, aglio
gather, raccogliere
gearing, sistemare
general store, drogheria
genial, geniale
get (become), diventare
get by, cavare
get hold of, procurare
geyser, scaldabagno
glance, sguardo, occhiata
glass, bicchiere, vetro
go, going to, andare
go away! via!
go on, su, senza
go out, salire
go to, recarsi
go to bed, coricarsi
go to get, prendere
go up, salire
goal, gol
goalkeeper, portiere
good deal, parecchio
Good Heavens! Oh Dio!
good job, meno
goose, oca
gooseberry, uva
gossip, chiacchierare
grammar school, ginnasio
grape, uva
gravy, salsa, sugo
grease, grasso
greasing, ingrassaggio
green, verde
greengrocer, erbivendolo,
   fruttivendolo

grocer's, salsamenteria
grounds, motivo
grow, diventare
guichet, sportello
guide, guida
gymnasium, palestra

haberdasher, merciaio
hacksaw, utensile
hair, pelo
hair-brush, spazzola
hairdresser, parrucchiere
half, mezzo
half-back, mediano
ham, prosciutto
hammer, lancio, martello
hand, mano
handle, manico, maniglia
handlebars, manubrio
hang out clothes, sciacquare
happen, capitare
hard up, secco
hasten, sbrigarsi
have it done, fare
hazel nut, nocciola
head, testa
headlight, proiettore, faro
head office, sede
headphone, cuffia
heads or tails, testa
hear, sentire
heart (at), fondo
heat, batteria; riscaldare
heater, stufa
heap, mucchio
Heaven's sake, carità
thank Heaven, male
hedge, siepe
hello, pronto; ciao
help, aiutare
here, ecco; ci
herring, aringa
high jump, saltare
high school, ginnasio
highway patrol, poliziotto
hinge, cardine
hint, insinuare
hit, colpire
honey, miele

hook, gancio
hooter, avvisatore
hop, step and jump, saltare
horn, corno
horrible, schifo
horror, racchia
hors d'œuvres, antipasto
horse-power, cavalli
horse races, corse ippiche
hose, tubo
hotel, albergo
hot-plate, forno
how are you? stare
how d'you do? piacere
however, comunque, però
how long? volere
how on earth? mai
hub, mozzo
hurdles, ostacoli
hurry, sbrigarsi
hurt, fare
hyphen, tratto

I say, sentire
ice, ghiaccio
ice-cream, gelateria
idea, idea
if only, magari
ignition, accensione
ignore, ignorare
imagine, capirai; figurarsi
immediately, subito
impression, colpo
impudent, sfrontato
index, scheda; indice
indicator, indicatore
indifferent, indifferente
individual, tizio
ink, inchiostro
inner tube, camera
insert, inserire
instead, invece
intention, scopo
international, nazionale
inverted commas, virgola
invoice, fattura
iron, stirare
ironmongery, casalinghi
isn't it? vero

jack, cric
jam, conserva, marmellata
javelin, giavellotto
jelly, gelatina
jersey, maglia
jet, getto, spruzzatore
jeweller's, gioielleria
job, posto
joint, giunto
judgment, sentenza
jug, caraffa
juice, sugo
jump, saltare
just, appunto, giusto, pure
just as well, male, meno
just fancy, figurarsi
just in case, mai
just tell me, poco

keep cool, sangue freddo
ketchup, pomodoro
kettle, bollitore
key, chiave; tastiera
keyhole, serratura
kick, calcio
kid, scherzo
kidnap, rubare
kidneys, rognoni
kill, uccidere
kiln, forno
kiosk, edicola
kitchen, cucina
kitchen sink, lavandino
knife, coltello
knit, fare
knob, manopola
knock down, atterrare
knock off, fregare
knows his onions, gamba

lack, mancanza
ladies, signore
lamb, agnello
lamp, lampada
lane, corsia
last straw, mancare
late, ritardo
lately, ultimamente
laundry, bucato
leading, in vantaggio

leaf, foglio
leak, via
lease, affittare
leather goods, pelletteria
leave it to me, ci
leave off, smettere
lecture, conferenza
leek, porro
leg, gamba
lemon, limone
lentils, lenticchie
let him have it, dai
let it go at that, perdere
let's see, vediamo
lettuce, lattuga
level crossing, passaggio
lever, leva
licence, patente
lie, bugia
lift, passaggio
light, fanale, luce
lighthouse, faro
like this, così
limp, zoppicare
line, riga
line-up, formazione
linseed oil, olio
liquid, liquido
list, elenco
little, poco
live, campare
liver, fegato
lobster, aragosta
lock, serratura
logical, logico
long jump, saltare
long time, pezzo
lottery, lotteria
lubrication, lubrificazione
lubricator, lubricatore
luggage rack, portabagagli
lunatic, matto

machine, macchina
mackerel, scombro
mad, matto, pazzo
mad on, pazzo
magneto, magnete
make, fare
make ends meet, pane

make haste, sbrigarsi
make it snappy, svelto
make sick, schifo
make up mind, decidersi
magazine, rivista
male, maschio
manner, modo
manufacture, fabbricare
Marathon, maratona
mark you, ecco
marmalade, marmellata
marrow, midollo
masseur, massaggiatore
mass production, serie
mat, stuoino
match, gara, partita; fiammifero
matter, faccenda
mayor, sindaco
meal, pasto
means, mezzo
meat, carne
meeting, riunione
mess, pasticcio, guaio
message, comunicazione
messenger, fattorino, messaggio
meter, contatore
milk, latte
Milky Way, via
milometer, contachilometri
mind, però; mente
mint, menta
mirror, specchio
mishap, disgrazia
miss, mancanza
missing, mancare
model, indossatrice, modello
moment, momento
money, soldi
money order, vaglia
mood, umore
mop, radazza
more, ancora
more or less, meno
moreover, pure
motor, motore
motor-bike, motociclo
motor scooter, motore
mudguard, parabrezza

mushroom, fungo
must, bisognare
mustard, senape
mutton, montone

nail, chiodo
namely, cioè
necessarily, forza
need, bisognare, occorrere
needle, ago
neutral, folle
never, mai
nevertheless, eppure
news, novità
nice, simpatico
nimble, svelto
(he's) no square, gamba
noise, chiasso
noisy, noioso
nonsense, bugia
not at all, niente, modo
not fail to, mancare
not in slightest, mica
not know, ignorare
not matter, importare
not realize, ignorare
not so bad, mica, male
not stop from, togliere
not turn up, mancare
note, appunto
nothing, nulla
nothing to be done, niente
notice, accorgersi
noticeable, sensibile
notorious, notorietà
now and then, tanto
nuclear warhead, testa
number plate, targa
nut, noce; dado
nutmeg, noce

object, scopo
obtain, procurare
occur, occorrere
oculist, oculista
of course, senza
of late, ultimamente
off, via
office, ufficio

oil, olio; benzina
oil-can, oliatore
oil seal, tenuta
oil sump, coppa
O.K., andare, bene
olive, oliva
olive oil, olio
on point of, lì lì
on subject of, proposito
on the spot, posto
one, unico
one-way, unico
onion, cipolla
only, unico
opponent, avversario
or else, oppure
orange, arancia
ordinary, ordinario
origin, radice
out of order, guasto
outfitter's, abbigliamento
oven, forno
overbearing, prepotente
overflow pipe, scarico
own, proprio
oyster, ostrica

palace, palazzo
pan, teglia
pane, lastra
paper, carta
paper clip, fermaglio
paper-knife, tagliacarte
paragraph, paragrafo
park, parcheggiare
parking meter, parcheggiare
parsley, prezzemolo
parsnip, pastinaca
partridge, pernice
pass exam, laurea
passage, passaggio
passport, passaporto
patent, patente
patience, pazienza
pavement, marciapiede
pea, pisello
peach, pesca
peanut, nocciola
pear, pera

pedal, pedale
pedantic, pignolo
peephole, sguardo
pen nib, pennino
pencil, matita
penthouse, attico
pepper, pepe
performance, spettacolo
perhaps, eventualmente, magari
permission, permesso
peroxide, acqua
pet shop, uccelleria
petrol, benzina
petrol tank, serbatoio
pharmacy, farmacia
pheasant, fagiano
pickled, marinato
pickles, salamoia
picture, quadro
pie, pasticcio
piece, pezzo
pig, maiale
pigeon, piccione
pile, mucchio
pillow, guanciale
pin, spillo
pinch (steal), fregare
pineapple, ananasso
pipe, tubo; condotta
piston, stantuffo
piston ring, segmento
place, posto
plaice, passerino
plate, piatto
play, commedia; toccare; giocare
player, giocare
pleasant, simpatico
please, piacere, prego
pliers, pinze
plug, tappo; spina
plug in, inserire
plum, prugna
plumber, idraulico
point, caso; punto
pole vault, saltare
police station, posto; questura
policeman, poliziotto
polish, lucidare

polite, educato
pork, maiale
porter, palazzo
possibly, eventualmente
post, imbucare
post office, ufficio
postal order, vaglia
postcard, cartolina
postmark, timbro
pot, pentola; barattolo
potato, patata
power, potenza
practice, esercizio
prawn, gambero
precisely, appunto, proprio
(at) present, attualmente
pretty, carino
prevention, preventivo
pride oneself on, piccarsi
produce, fabbricare
professional, professionista
promenade, lungomare
proper, giusto
prove right, ragione
prove to be, risultare
pudding, budino
pull the leg, girare
pump, pompa
pumpkin, zucca
punch, colpire; punzonare
puncture, forare, puntura, bucatura
purpose, scopo
(on) purpose, proposito
purse, borsa
push, spingere
put, mettere
put a sock in it, smettere
put out, spegnere; fastidio

quarrel, litigare
quench, togliere
question, questione
quick, svelto
quince, cotogna
quite, piuttosto
quite right too, ragione

rabbit, coniglio
racket, chiasso
race, corse
radiator, radiatore
radiator cap, tappo
radiator grill, cuffia
radish, radice
rag, straccio
raisin, uva
rape, rubare
rasher, fetta
rasp, utensile
raspberry, lampone
rate (at any), modo, comunque
rate of exchange, cambiare
rather, anzi; piuttosto
razor, rasoio
reading, lettura
ready, pronto
realize, accorgersi, rendersi
really, proprio
rear window, lunetta
reason, motivo
recently, ultimamente
recognized, valevole
recommend, raccomandare
record, disco; primato
record holder, stabilire
referee, arbitro
refreshment, rinfresco
refrigerator, frigorifero
register, raccomandare
Registry Office, anagrafe
relay race, staffetta
reluctantly, malincuore
remain, rimanere
rent, affittare, pigione
repair, riparazione
reply, rispondere
reserve, riserva
reservoir, serbatoio
rest, reggersi
restaurant, ristorante, trattoria
result, risultare
reverse, marcia
review, criticare
ribbon, nastro
rice, riso

ridiculous, buffo
right, ragione
right away, subito
ring, squillo
rinse, sciacquare
rise, salire
road, via
roast, arrosto
rob, rubare
roof tile, tegola
Rome dialect, romanesco
room, posto; camera, stanza
rot, stupidaggine
round, ripresa
round the bend, proprio
row, chiasso
rowing, canottaggio
rub, fregare
rub out, cancellare
rubber stamp, timbro
rubbish, bugia, stupidaggine, immondizia
ruffled, sconosciuto
ruler, riga

safe, cassaforte
safety pin, spillo
safety razor, rasoio
sage, salvia
sail, vela
sailing, vela
salad, insalata
salmon, salmone
salt, sale
salute, salutare
sardine, sardina
sauce, salsa
saucepan, casseruola
saucy, sfrontato
sausage, salsiccia
saw, sega
say hello, salutare
scale, scala
scalpel, scalpello
screw, vite
screwdriver, cacciavite
scissors, forbici
sea-power, potenza
season, stagione
seat, sedile

second, secondo
secondary school, ginnasio
secretary, segretario
see again, rivedere
self-starter, mettere
semi-colon, due punti
send, spedire
sensible, sensato
sensitive, sensibile
sentence, sentenza
series, serie
serves you right, bene
set, serie
several, diverso
shade, sfumatura
shake hands, mano
shambles, macello
shame, vergogna
sharpen, appuntare
shave, rasoio
shelf, scaffale
sheet, foglio; lenzuolo
shirt shop, camiceria
shock, sciocco
shock absorber, ammortizzatore
shoe brush, spazzola
shoemaker, calzolaio
shop, bottega, negozio
shop assistant, commessa
(in) short, insomma
short (person), tappo
short time ago, poco
shorthand, stenografia
shot, lancio
shove, spingere
shovel, pala
show, spettacolo
show-off, fusto
shower-bath, doccia
shrimp, gamberetto
shroud, cuffia
shut up, stare; piantala
silencer, silenziatore
silk, seta
silly, buffo, sciocco
single, unico
sink (kitchen), lavandino
sir, signore; commendatore
sirloin, lombata

sitting room, stanza
skid, slittare
skins, pelletteria
sleep tight, sogni
slice, fetta
slide, scivolare
slip, scivolare
slippery, sdrucciolevole
sly (on the), nascosto
smoked, affumicato
snack, spuntino
so, pure, quindi
social services, servizi
socket, presa
sole, unico; sogliola
sooner or later, poi
sorry, dispiace
sort, razza
sound, suonare
soup, brodo, minestra, zuppa
space bar, sbarra
spaghetti, pastasciutta
spanner, chiave
spare, di ricambio, scorta
sparkling wine, spumante
speaking, sono
speech, discorso
speedometer, tachimetro
spinach, spinaci
spiral staircase, scala
spit, sputare
spoon, cucchiaio
spring, molla
spring-board, trampolino
sprint, scattare
sprout, cavolini
squash, spremuta
squeegee, radazza
squid, seppia
staircase, scala
(at) stake, ballo, palio
star (cinema), diva
stark, staring mad, matto
stationer's, cartoleria
stay, rimanere
steal, rubare
steeplechase, siepe
stencil, clichè
stepladder, scala
stew, stufato

stick, attaccare
stick in, ficcare
still, ancora, comunque, eppure
stock, scorta
Stock Exchange, Borsa
stop, fermare
stop it, smettere
stopper, tappo
store, magazzino, scorta
stove, stufa, forno, cucina
strap-handle, pendaglio
strawberry, fragola
strength, forza
strike, scioperare
string, spago
strip-tease, spogliatrice
stroll, lungomare
stuff, roba
stump, mozzicone
stupid, sciocco
stupidity, stupidaggine
style, stile
success, successo
such, tanto
suddenly, tratto
sugar, zucchero
sugar-basin, zucchero
sugar beet, zucchero
sugar cane, zucchero
suggest, insinuare
suitable, giusto
suitcase, valigia
suits me, convenire
sun screen, parabrezza
sunset, tramonto
sun tan, tintarella
supper, cena
supporter, tifoso
sweet, dolce
switch, interruttore
switch off, spegnere
switch on, accendere
swim, nuotare
swimming-pool, nuotare
syndicate, sindacato

table, tavola
tailor's, sartoria
take advantage, sfruttare
take away, togliere

take hint, insinuare
take life, togliere
take mickey, girare
take note, appunto
take off, togliere
take place, verificare
take seat, accomodare
take to, pigliare
tank, serbatoio
tap, rubinetto
tape, traguardo, nastro
tape measure, metro, nastro
tape recorder, registratore
tea service, servizio da tè
tea tray, vassoio
team, squadra
teapot, teiera
teaspoon, cucchiaio
teaspoonful, cucchiaio
telephone directory, elenco, guida
telephone exchange, centralino
television, televisore
tell truth, vero
temper, umore
terminus, capo
terrible, disastro
terribly, morire
thank you, grazie
that's all, ecco
that's right, già
that's that, ecco
that's to say, cioè
then, poi, allora
there (is), ci; ecco
therefore, quindi
thimble, ditale
thing, cosa, roba
thingummy, coso
think (just), figurarsi
thorny, spinoso
thread, filo, vite
throttle, farfalla
throw, lanciare, buttare
thrust, spingere
tight, brillo, parecchio, sbornia
tighten, vite
time-table, orario
tin, scatola

tip, mancia
tired, fiacca
tobacconist, tabaccaio
toilet paper, carta
token, gettone
tomato, pomodoro
tongue, lingua
too big for boots, prepotente
tool, utensile
toothbrush, spazzola
top gear, presa
topic, argomento
toss up, croce
touch, toccare
Tour de France, girare, ciclismo
track, pista
traffic cop, poliziotto
train, allenare
transmission, trasmissione
tray, vassoio
tread, battistrada
tree, albero
tremendous, tremendo
tricky, spinoso
trip, gita
trolley-bus, filobus
trouble, guaio
trout, trota
true, vero
trumpet, tromba
Tube, Metropolitana
tube, tubo
tunny, tonno
turbot, rombo
turkey, tacchino
turn, girare
turn (my), toccare
turn out, svolgere
turn out to be, risultare
turnip, rapa
turpentine, acqua
type, scrivere, battere
typist, dattilografa
tyre, gomma, pneumatico

ultimately, ultimamente
umpire, arbitro
uncover, scoprire
undersized, tappo

understand, capire
unfortunately, purtroppo
unknown, sconosciuto
unless, meno
unload, scarica
unruffled, sconosciuto
upholstery, tappezzeria
upset, fastidio
up to (someone), toccare
up to a point, punto
us, ci
usual, solito
utilities, servizi

vacuum cleaner, aspirapolvere
valid, valevole
valve, valvola
vanilla, vainiglia
various, diverso
vegetable, verdura, legume
Venus, venire
vest, maglia
vice, utensile
vinegar, aceto
V.I.P., pezzo
vision, visione
vulgar, ordinario

wait, attendere
walk, marcia
want, volere
wash, lavare
washbasin, lavabo
washer (tap), rondella
washing, bucato
washing machine, lavatrice
waste paper, carta
waste paper basket, cestino
water, acqua
watertight, tenuta
water-cress, crescione
water-melon, cocomero
water-polo, palla
way, modo; via
weak point, debole

weight, peso
we'll see, vediamo
well, allora, bene, ebbene,
 dunque
well-mannered, educato
wet, bagnato
whale oil, olio
what? cosa
what's come over? venire
what's eating? prendere
what's-his-name, coso, non so
what's more, pure
why? ragione
wide, largo
win, vincere
wind, scirocco; tramontana
window, finestrino
windscreen, parabrezza
windscreen-wiper, tergicristallo
wine, vino
wing, ala
winter sports, sport
wire, filo
wish, augurio; voglia
with pleasure, volentieri
within ace of, pelo
without, senza
without doubt, senza
without fail, senza
witty, spiritoso
wool, lana
worry, preoccupare
worth it, valere
would you mind telling me?
 togliere
wrench, utensile
wretch, disgrazia
writing desk, scrivania
writing paper, carta

yellow, giallo
yes, già
yet, ancora, eppure, però

zip fastener, lampone